T0298710

"I am not aware of another book that makes as strong and well-founded a claim for the relevance of humanistic thought on discussions of digital disinformation and bias usually dominated by social scientists, computer scientists, and journalists. A very original work that brings the long history of European hermeneutical thought to bear on online trust, skepticism, and dialogue in today's 'platform hermeneutics.' And the book is great fun too in its inventive use of AI and machine learning to analyze case studies on Tumblr, Reddit, and elsewhere."

Alan Liu, *Distinguished Professor, University of California Santa Barbara, USA*

"In the world of digital communication, researchers – and ordinary users alike – have to deal with a situation of information overload. The abundance of data is certainly a great opportunity for in-depth knowledge of social processes, but the risk of 'drowning' in it, is ever-present. This insightful book by Inge van de Ven and Lucie Chateau discusses how scholars of digital culture and society can extricate themselves from this information abundance trap, by recuperating the hermeneutic tradition of close reading, qualitative analysis and in-depth interpretation, and deploying it to address the new materials of contempoary digital culture: tweets, online videos, internet memes, conversations of all sorts. A recommended reading for those searching for methods to understand the symbolisms and meanings of contemporary digital cultures."

Paolo Gerbaudo, *Senior Researcher in Social Science, Complutense University in Madrid, Spain*

Digital Culture and the Hermeneutic Tradition

In our information age, deciding what sources and voices to trust is a pressing matter. There seems to be a surplus of both trust and distrust in and on platforms, both of which often amount to having your mindset remain the same. Can we move beyond this dichotomy toward new forms of intersubjective dialogue? This book revaluates the hermeneutic tradition for the digital context. Today, hermeneutics has migrated from a range of academic approaches into a plethora of practices in digital culture at large. We propose a 'scaled reading' of such practices: a reconfiguration of the hermeneutic circle, using different tools and techniques of reading. We demonstrate our digital-hermeneutic approach through case studies including toxic depression memes, the Johnny Depp/Amber Heard trial, and r/changemyview. We cover three dimensions of hermeneutic practice: suspicion, trust, and dialogue. This book is essential reading for (under)graduate students in digital humanities and literary studies.

Inge van de Ven is Associate Professor of Culture Studies at Tilburg School of Humanities and Digital Sciences. She was Marie Curie Global Fellow at UC Santa Barbara and Junior Core Fellow at the Institute of Advanced Study, Budapest. Her monograph *Big Books in Times of Big Data* was published in 2019. Articles appeared in journals such as *European Journal of English Studies*, *Medical Humanities*, *Narrative*, *Digital Humanities Quarterly*, *Celebrity Studies*, and *Journal for Creative Behavior*.

Lucie Chateau is a media scholar and digital culture researcher interested in meme aesthetics. She recently finished her PhD entitled *Anxious Aesthetics: Memes and Alienation in Digital Capitalism*, which investigated the subversive potential of aesthetics online. Her work has looked at a variety of meme genres such as depression memes, anti-capitalist memes, and climate change memes and argues we are witnessing the emergence of experimental aesthetic forms that negotiate new forms of representation under digital capitalism.

Routledge Focus on Literature

For more information about this series, please visit: https://www.routledge.com/
Routledge-Focus-on-Literature/book-series/RFLT

Digital Culture and the Hermeneutic Tradition

Suspicion, Trust, and Dialogue

Inge van de Ven and Lucie Chateau

Routledge
Taylor & Francis Group
NEW YORK AND LONDON

First published 2025
by Routledge
605 Third Avenue, New York, NY 10158

and by Routledge
4 Park Square, Milton Park, Abingdon, Oxon, OX14 4RN

Routledge is an imprint of the Taylor & Francis Group, an informa business

© 2025 Inge van de Ven and Lucie Chateau

ISBN: 978-1-032-44562-5 (hbk)
ISBN: 978-1-032-44564-9 (pbk)
ISBN: 978-1-003-37279-0 (ebk)

DOI: 10.4324/9781003372790

Typeset in Times New Roman
by codeMantra

Contents

Introduction

The Problem of Epistemic Vigilance

In our current information age, where messages rapidly proliferate across different media, deciding what sources and voices to trust and pay attention to is a pressing matter. Trust forms the basis of social life, since most of our knowledge comes from testimony of others, which can only happen when we trust these others to be competent and sincere. At the same time, it can be lucrative for humans to deceive each other in order to further our own well-being. Believing someone or something, therefore, always entails a risk. Over the course of evolution, humans have developed skills to distinguish trustworthy from untrustworthy communicators and mitigate the risk of being (deliberately or inadvertently) misinformed. To ensure that communication remains to our advantage and relatively honest, Sperber et al. (2010) postulate, we have a range of cognitive mechanisms at our disposal for the evaluation of information: mechanisms for 'epistemic vigilance' that help us calibrate trust and vigilance. These warrant openness, meaning we can accept most beneficial messages while being vigilant enough to reject harmful messages. In any communicative act, sender and receiver have to put in some effort in exchange for a benefit. The communicator's effort lies in performing the utterance; the receiver's effort in paying attention and interpreting. For the communicator, the benefit in return is the intended effect the utterance produces in the addressee (e.g., to convince them that something is the case, change their beliefs), regardless of whether it is true or false; for the receiver, the benefit is receiving true and relevant information. Both goals can be compatible but they rarely align perfectly. To warrant that communication remains overall beneficial to both parties, we need to calibrate trust. Trust is buttressed by active epistemic vigilance: we can be trusting *because* we are vigilant. Vigilance, Sperber et al. (2010) stress, is not distrust. It is opposed to blind trust, not trust.

Epistemic vigilance becomes especially urgent in today's digitalized societies where competing claims are plentiful and source information can be diffuse. How do we calibrate our (dis)trust when it comes to sources of information today, given limited resources of time and attention? There seems to

DOI: 10.4324/9781003372790-1

be a surplus of both trust and distrust in contemporary media culture. On the one hand, increasing polarization in culture means we can be deeply suspicious of others outside our ideological bubble, and trust in experts is waning in certain communities. Radicalizing content and the mainstreaming of conspiracy thought contribute to a deep-seated distrust of others and of *things as they seem*. On the other hand, we might place too much trust in the platforms that govern and structure our online lives. We rely on algorithms to organize our lives and make decisions for us. We fall prey to confirmation bias and echo chambers, which we might characterize as an overly trusting attitude toward (human and/or technological) others.

Social media platforms often seem designed to afford ever so many ways to connect us with those who think the same and to close off a conversation with those who don't. They come with a complete vocabulary for this, including terms like *blocked, unfollowed, unsubscribed, unfriended, reported.* A meme (Figure 0.1) that circulates around the time of writing this parodies such phrases through overuse, showing how commonplace and meaningless they have become in Twitter-style discourse: "some of y'all I don't know who

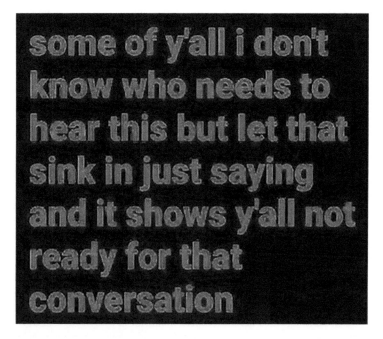

Figure 0.1 A meme that parodies polarizing discourse on X (formerly known as Twitter).

needs to hear this but let that sink in just saying and it shows y'all not ready for that conversation." It seems that online, we are mostly trying to legitimize our own truth by winning the trust of others.

The Bird Is Freed': Issues of Trust in Online Public Spheres

But how do we determine whom to trust online? Do we know *how* to trust? At the time of writing, billionaire Elon Musk of Tesla and SpaceX fame has just bought the platform Twitter for 44 billion dollars. Twitter, now renamed X, is one of the world's most influential social networks. It has a significant impact on how news is circulated and how people form opinions. Among its 450 million users are public figures such as politicians, scientists, and academics. One thing that X has always struggled with is the potential for misinformation to spread like wildfire on the platform, which has come under attack for giving its official "verified" status to a white supremacist and other controversial figures. Musk, who had been a renowned member of the platform for years, decided to fix this. He announced this purchase with a characteristic tweet: "the bird is freed."[1] According to him, his noble motive for the immense investment was that he wanted to make X "the most accurate source of information about the world."[2] To advertisers, he promised that it would no longer be "a Free-for-All Hellscape, where anything can be said without any consequences" (Haggin & Vranica, 2022). But the way he went about it had dire repercussions.

In order to understand what happened, you have to know that content moderation is X's weakest point. On such a global platform, where anybody with an internet connection can create an account and have access to a global network of other tweeters, malicious intent is rife. Abusive tweets, calls for bullying and threats, as well as numerous spam accounts have been part of the difficult landscape that has given X a bad reputation over the years. To solve these problems, Musk launched a revamp of X's verification process in the form of a paid subscription. Under this new scheme, users of the platform would pay eight dollars a month for the verified checkmark to appear next to their name. Previously, public figures who enjoyed the privileges of having their identities 'verified' on the platform did not have to pay for it. At the same time, it had been unclear how the platform went about deciding who had earned the right to be verified and who had not. The verified status was designed to authenticate identity and voice, to show that an account rightfully belonged to the person the username displayed (so the person behind the handle @realDonaldTrump was... *really* Donald Trump). For politicians, public figures, scientists, and academics, verification was conventional and interlinked with the other attributes expected of public figures: they had to be accessible, transparent, reachable. However, the initial ambition of identification (to connote authenticity) quickly became misinterpreted as a *sign of influence*. Seeing a blue checkmark next to an account's username came to be associated with importance or expertise (regardless of topic, field, or discipline) and made the verified user's voice more relevant than others.'

Under Musk's new scheme, a new process of verification relied solely on whether someone was willing and able to pay eight dollars to joke on the internet. As it turned out, many were. This launched a whole new onslaught of trolling and satirical accounts, the very thing that Musk wanted to crack down on. Within hours of the new "Twitter Blue"[3] being rolled out, parody accounts sprung out of the woodwork and began tweeting under their new "verified" identities. This led to impersonations of political figures: former US president George W. Bush supposedly admitted to missing the Iraq war, health care provider Eli Lilly claimed they were making insulin free, and brands like Chiquita confessed to having overthrown governments. Financial consequences ranged from small to major, with Eli Lilly stock dropping by more than 4%. For hours, chaos reigned on the platform. With a full name and blue verification tick, it is easy to overlook the fake handle (@). The tick, visual signifier of importance and influence, had already been cemented as a marker of authenticity for years on the platform. Though the process of obtaining the marker had changed, what it signified remained the same. Under the albeit flawed previous scheme, proof of identity was the logic of verification. However, the parameters for verification now had a new logic: pay, and you own. Musk's passion project crashed and burned. Twitter Blue came to a full stop a few days after it was introduced. Its spectacular failure shows us the complexities of verification and fact-checking online. For indeed, this problem is not unique to X. Online social networking sites have become places to not just talk to our friends, as in the early days of Facebook, but also have direct access to our idols, political representatives, and the brands behind the products we consume. And, of course, they want something in exchange: *our attention*.

Social networking sites have redefined what it means to participate in the public sphere. They have encouraged the idea that access to others is a fundamental egalitarian principle. By providing a space for this, platforms like X have assigned themselves major roles in today's politics. Everyone has a say in this version of the digital public sphere, but some voices are louder and thus have more reach than others. Platforms have not only changed where and how conversations happen: they have changed the parameters of conversation itself. Can conversation happen when we are not sure of the other's identity? In these cases, who or what defines what is true, what we can believe? We land back at the question we started with: how do we know whom to trust? In this book, we offer an overview of issues in online media related to questions of trust and objectivity–think of 'buzzwords' like algorithms, filter bubbles, echo chambers, skepticism, mis/disinformation, and post-truth. We make the claim that these are 'hermeneutic' problems, meaning they relate to the topic and study of *interpretation*. Hermeneutics allows us to bring the more subjective issue of trust and interpretation back into the equation in an age when we are constantly faced with the supposed objectivity of data.

Data Mythologies

When it comes to data, it is often suggested that we can bypass interpretation altogether. This is especially the case with big data: data which is too voluminous for traditional data-processing software that translates data into information. With big data, key issues like data capture, storage, transfer, analysis, and visualization as well as information privacy arise. The data ecosystem is therefore a wide set of practices that seek to make data useful for society. This is known as *datafication*: creating value from data. Data creates a world where quantification produces value and influences users' behaviors to create more data, which in turn creates more information, which in turn creates more value. The usage of big data in society hinges on the simple belief that human behavior and rationality can be reduced to a series of data points and that feeding these data points into a computational system will help the world function better. Big data is a form of predictive analytics that helps us more accurately foresee what will happen. The idea is that, if we have enough data about what has happened in the past and the parameters surrounding the data stay the same, meaning that the conditions in which the data can be applied has to correspond to the conditions in which data was harvested, the future must correspond to the past, then big data can help us do better in the future.

Technology and media scholars danah boyd and Kate Crawford (2012) urge us to demystify data as a way of perceiving the world, and to pay attention to its limitations. They point out that big data results from a particular technological imaginary which builds on a belief and trust in quantification and its potential for modeling reality. They call this the "mythology" of big data, "the widespread belief that large data sets offer a higher form of intelligence and knowledge that can generate insights that were previously impossible, with the aura of truth, objectivity, and accuracy" (662). Big data is believed to bypass representation and interpretation, and to refer directly to reality. In short, believing in data as a way to represent the world means believing in the *ideology* of data. José van Dijck (2014) calls this widespread belief in the objectivity of data *dataism*, and it implies a basic level of trust in the institutional agents that collect it from us. As Angela Wu (2020) writes in *Data & Society*, platform data do not provide a direct window onto human behavior. Rather, they are records of how we behave under platforms' influence. Relying blindly on data has many dangerous side effects for our cognitive capacity, such as forgetting our ability to critically interrogate and investigate the world around us. But it is important to note that data also encompasses an emergent set of practices, meaning that experimenting with ways to interact with data can also be creative and critical.

Whereas big data has thus led to dreams of objectivity, on the other side of the objectivity/subjectivity binary, algorithms curate highly subjective environments. Algorithms are technical, material, experiential, and affective processes that structure our digital experiences. Computationally speaking, they are a set of instructions for a computer program to complete a task. They steer our behavior by structuring the spaces where we interact. Algorithms coordinate nudging (the practice of influencing decision-making) and gamification (rewarding users for participation or certain behaviors). The sense that content on a site is completely tailored to your interests and regularly refreshed, besides adding to online platforms' addictive nature, means it becomes easy to create an experience wherein one's views are merely confirmed rather than challenged. One of the main impediments to understanding each other online is ideological segregation. The ideologically cohesive spaces created by recommendation and personalization algorithms are often called filter bubbles (Pariser, 2011), and we write more about this issue of filtering, and the so-called 'echo chambers' it shapes, in Chapter 3. For now, it is important to understand that platforms can be seen as creating an environment for interactions with *people who think like you*.

As this brief overview of current developments in datafication drives home, we seem to be suspended between the seemingly objective and highly subjective. We are told that more data lead to a more comprehensive and less subjective picture of reality. Yet, precisely because of an abundance of information that is available to us at all times and through different channels, new ways of filtering this information for us lead to selective exposure to content. In digital humanities, the tension between the subjective and the objective plays out as an ongoing preoccupation with the lure of 'dataism' or the Big Data Myth, the seeming objectivity of the N = all perspective, versus the limited, situated, specific horizon of the human researcher. In this book, we argue that this tension between the seemingly objective and subjective content plays out as a problem of choosing between (often uncritical or blind) trust in media and likeminded others, and (often unwarranted and unhelpful) distrust of people who think differently.

Intersubjectivity and Interpretation

A contemporary challenge in academia and online culture therefore lies in moving beyond these pillars and understanding epistemologies and viewpoints that differ from our own. To this end, we should understand truths as environmentally constituted and culturally situated. Are there ways to move beyond the dichotomy of (uncritical) trust and (unwarranted) distrust—both of which often amount to having your mindset remain the same—toward new forms of intersubjective dialogue in online culture? How does dialogism come about on public platforms, and does it allow for calibrations of trust and distrust or skepticism? How, as students and researchers, can we intervene without pretending to stand apart from, or hover Godlike above, online platforms and their contents?

In this context, the importance of media literacy education has been stressed, as a field that could help train critical readers and viewers who are able to distinguish truths from falsities. The Center for Media Literacy defines media literacy as "a framework to access, analyze, evaluate, create and participate with messages in a variety of forms — from print to video to the Internet."[4] Students are taught to critically question sources and consider the sender's motivations. However, danah boyd (2018) has expressed discomfort with media literacy when this means having students do 'the research' for themselves, which in practice often means they rely on google and use the top-ranked sources. She argues that this places unreasonable demands on individuals by making them responsible for truth-finding, which might reinforce the idea that there is a single truth out there to be discovered—with paranoia, extremism, and polarization as possible results. Young people especially form a risk group in this mediascape marked by doubt and skepticism. They tend to be inclined to challenge authority and seek alternative explanations; some adolescents take refuge in extremist online communities.

As educators and students in the humanities and social sciences, we thus face the challenge of understanding the epistemological differences between groups in society. This finally brings us to the topic of this book: hermeneutics, which will be properly introduced in Chapter 1, is the study of interpretation, and it inquires into the conditions of possibility for understanding. In its historical context, hermeneutics as a philosophical and scholarly tradition came about as an answer to problems of mediating between concepts of objective reality and the subjective nature of human experience. After the 'Copernican Turn' established by Kant's transcendental idealism and its reversal of the positions of knowing subject and known object, hermeneutic philosophies intended to grapple with the problem of the limited and perspectivist nature of human subjectivity by proposing a mode of intersubjectivity, of transferring oneself to the standpoint of others. Textual mediation was central to communicating this intersubjectivity, and hermeneutics became a central approach in literary studies. Rather than postulating objectivity or subjectivity as a basis for knowledge, hermeneutics understands experience as *intersubjective*. In a sense, the world is intersubjective: as subjects or individuals we share the same world and make meaning out of it. Experience is always shared, albeit filtered through our individual horizons. We think that the intersubjectivity that hermeneutics promotes, especially in Gadamer's (2004) notion of a fusion of horizons (discussed in Chapters 1 and 4), could help us get beyond the current polarization that marks digital culture, which we characterized as an excess of both trust and distrust. With this book, we make a case for revaluing and reevaluating the hermeneutic tradition in philosophy and literary studies for the digital context, based on hermeneutics' mediating role and emphasis on intersubjectivity, beyond any simplified binary of objectivity and subjectivity.

Our own approach to hermeneutic interventions into digital culture, which will be outlined in more detail in the chapters to come, consists of a layered structure of elements that we reflect on when analyzing online media content:

Platforms: When we look at the platform itself as an environment for online communications, we need to keep in mind how the architecture of social media platforms have sociality built into them and how that effectively makes them environments that distribute control. Platform hermeneutics includes attention to the following elements:

- User Interface: How does the material structure of the platform (i.e., what it looks like, including any homepage, feed, user, or profile page) set up the user's relationship to the platform? Does it allow for trackability of users? Does it allow for context to be easily decontextualized and recontextualized (i.e., edited and re-interpreted?)
- Affordances: What are the features and functions of the website such as liking, commenting, and sharing? What do they promote? Do they offer a collective or a connective space? Are all affordances perceptible or at some hidden?
- Governmentality: Policies and moderation affect what is posted on the platform. What are the rules and conventions set in place? Are the interventions of platform owners perceptible? How do users treat them? Algorithms also fall into this category since they structure and hierarchize content.
- Is the platform identity-based, pseudonymous, or anonymous?

Cultural practices: At this level, we ask how modes of self-expression are influenced by the platform: how do they set up relations between users and what dynamics do those relations create? This includes elements like:

- Authenticity (in the case of identity-based platforms): think about what does authenticity encourage: accountability, hegemony, curation of your online persona, identification with your digital avatar? Self-promotion?
- Subversion (in the case of pseudonymous or anonymous platforms): what does anonymity allow: provocation, incendiary or politically incorrect remarks, a chance to say something but not be held accountable? Playfulness?

Literacy: At the level of literacy, we ask what knowledge one needs to master to analyze the object. Are you encountering the text in its native environment, or has it originated in another context? Here, we can think of aspects like…

- Irony: Can the expression be considered sincere and taken at face-value or is it meant ironically, and how can we determine this, based on evidence? Is the original author of the text the one with ironic intent or has it been revisited and posted ironically? To whom would it read ironically and to whom would this not be ironic?

- Subculturality: Does the expression have a broad appeal? Does it contain reference to something that you are not familiar with? Is its vocabulary or visual register uncommon?

Our first chapter offers a detailed investigation of the hermeneutic framework and how it applies to digital technologies in general and digital literary studies in particular. In the next three chapters, two to four, follows a demonstration of this framework in a range of ways, structured according to three different dimensions of hermeneutic practice: suspicion, trust, and dialogue. Here, you will also find examples of how you can apply such a digital-hermeneutic approach to a number of case studies in online culture, including toxic memes about depression, the trial between Johnny Depp and Amber Heard, and the subreddit r/changemyview. We focus on online corpora, yet we approach the discourses in a literary manner, with an emphasis on stylistics, irony, ambiguities, et cetera. Because of the central role of ambiguity, layers of irony, unreliable narrators, and other 'literary' devices online, we 'read' these examples in online culture from a literary-hermeneutic perspective. Yet, we move beyond the linguistic bias of the hermeneutic tradition and focus on the analysis of visual images on different scales alongside, and intertwining with, the digital-textual. But first, in the next chapter, we will explain why we consider this top-to-bottom approach an important feature of a hermeneutic approach to online culture. Materiality and relationality are crucial aspects here, since the online environment is not some indifferent, meaningless plane but, on the contrary, meaning is in the environment itself. This method places us in conversation with the structure that hosts the texts we want to analyze. Its concepts are ways to question how we interpret discourse on a platform when we keep in mind its architecture and the modes of sociality built into it.

Notes

1 Elon Musk, October 18th, 2022 https://twitter.com/elonmusk/status/158584108043 1321088.
2 Elon Musk, November 7th 2022 https://twitter.com/elonmusk/status/158941365319 0938624.
3 X was still known as Twitter at the time.
4 https://medialiteracynow.org/challenge/what-is-media-literacy/.

References

boyd, d. (2018, March 9). You Think You Want Media Literacy... Do You? *Zephoria*. https://www.zephoria.org/thoughts/archives/2018/03/09/you-think-you-want-media-literacy-do-you.html
boyd, d., & Crawford, K. (2012). Critical Questions for Big Data: Provocations for a Cultural, Technological, and Scholarly Phenomenon. *Information, Communication & Society*, 15(5), 662–679.

Center for Media Literacy. The Current State of Media & Children. Retrieved 13 September 2023, https://medialiteracynow.org/challenge/what-is-media-literacy/

van Dijck, J. (2014). Datafication, Dataism and Dataveillance: Big Data between Scientific Paradigm and Ideology. *Surveillance & Society*, 12(2), 197–208.

Gadamer, H. G. (2004). *Truth and Method*, 2nd ed. Trans. D. G. Marshall. London & New York: Continuum.

Haggin, P., & Vranica, S. (2022, October 28). Elon Musk Says Twitter Won't Be 'Free-for-All Hellscape,' Addressing Advertisers' Concern. *Wall Street Journal*. https://www.wsj.com/articles/elon-musk-will-face-an-early-twitter-challenge-preventing-advertiser-flight-11666871828

Musk, E. [@elonmusk] (2022, October 18). *The Bird Is Freed*. [Tweet]. Twitter. https://twitter.com/elonmusk/status/1585841080431321088

Musk, E. [@elonmusk] (2022, November 7). *Twitter Needs to Become By Far the Most Accurate Source of Information About the World. That's Our Mission*. [Tweet]. Twitter. https://twitter.com/elonmusk/status/1589413653190938624

Pariser, E. (2011). *The Filter Bubble: How the New Personalized Web Is Changing What We Read and How We Think*. London: Penguin.

Sperber, D., et al. (2010). Epistemic Vigilance. *Mind & Language*, 25(4), 359–393.

Wu, A. (2020, July 28). How Not to Know Ourselves. *Data & Society*. https://medium.com/datasociety-points/how-not-to-know-ourselves-5227c185569

1 The Familiar and the Strange

Rethinking Hermeneutics for the Digital

This chapter lays the groundwork of bringing the history of hermeneutic thought to bear on problems of trust, skepticism, and dialogue in contemporary online media. We make a case for a revaluation of hermeneutic theory in the Humanities in the context of present-day online public spheres and digital literary and media studies. We explain the relevance of hermeneutical approaches to issues surrounding trust in the information age. Despite recent theories of literature and culture that claim to move beyond, or go against the hermeneutic enterprise, we argue, hermeneutics is central to a range of contemporary practices in digital humanities and literary studies. But not just that: today, it has migrated from a range of approaches in academia, to a plethora of practices in online culture at large that warrant scholarly reflection. Rather than the historical, cultural, or geographical gaps centralized in the canon of hermeneutic thought, we argue, today we are faced with a polarization in online culture that takes on ideological and epistemological terms. We revise and reposition hermeneutical thought itself for the digital, so-called "postcritical" or post-hermeneutic age and make a case for its relevance in relation to the problems of digital trust, fake news, and bias that we outlined in the introduction to this book. We argue that hermeneutics today has come to function as a calibration of trust and distrust—of content, of authors, and of platforms. We present a review of existing studies that engage with hermeneutics and the digital, and then present our own approach in this book. This approach consists of a 'scaled reading' of cultural objects, oscillating from the whole dataset to a sample and describing the circular motion of the hermeneutic circle.

A Short Introduction to the Hermeneutic Tradition

In classical antiquity, hermeneutics entailed the translation of authoritative texts by the poet who was deemed the interpreter of the gods. Ancient poetry was meant to be read *allegorically*, in a search for the real, figural meaning behind the literal letters of the text. In early Christianity, hermeneutics entailed the exegesis of the Old Testament. Both originary uses were marked by

DOI: 10.4324/9781003372790-2

a tension between the familiar and the strange, a gap between the text and its original context and the contemporary lifeworld. In folk etymology, hermeneutics is connected to Hermes, who was the son of Zeus and the messenger of the Greek gods. His task was to transfer the words of the gods to other people. He was a mediator, and in fact the first translator. Hermeneutics is about building bridges—about mediating between self and other, the familiar and the and strange. It is thus always in-between. "Interpretation would be impossible if expressions of life were completely strange. It would be unnecessary if nothing strange were in them" (Dilthey, 1966, 225).

In 1900, Wilhelm Dilthey proposed hermeneutics, as a counterpart to the natural sciences, as the defining method for the Humanities [*Geisteswissenschaften*]. In the late nineteenth century, with the rise of the natural sciences, the Humanities seemed to be forced into a competition with those disciplines that made use of more "objective" standards. As studies of human beings and all they make and do, the Humanities seemed to be hard-pressed to live up to such standards. Rather than entering into a competition and making the Humanities more objective, in this context, Dilthey (1966) famously introduced a distinction between *Erklären* (to explain) and *Verstehen* (to understand) as the crucial difference between both branches and their goals. Under the flag of the upcoming paradigm of positivism, the natural sciences engaged in explaining, which meant to subsume the particular under the universal according to certain laws, like cause and effect. The Humanities could not live up to this level of 'objectivity,' and, according to Dilthey, they should not try. Dilthey reasoned that its objects of study, namely products of the 'human spirit,' like art and literature, could not be explained in the same manner. They warranted a different approach, as they do not follow such laws. Rather than explaining, Humanities scholars must *understand*, which means making empathic sense of their objects and rendering particular phenomena understandable by placing them in their broad historical framework. Dilthey understood meaning as a movement from outside, or surface, to inside, or essence. A text printed in a book is very clearly an empirical object—ink on paper—but its meaning is far removed from that of ink that has accidentally been spilled on blotting paper. Crucial to the text is that it *means*: that it is a product of a human spirit with its own unique structure.

The German theologian Friedrich Schleiermacher was the first to attempt to turn biblical exegesis into a serious academic discipline. He famously called hermeneutics the "art of understanding" (1998 [1809], 73). In a break with traditions, he thereby announced that the hermeneutic approach did not just encompass the text, or *what* needed to be understood, but also, but more importantly, was to understand understanding *itself*. Hermeneutics began to refer to interpretation and the study of interpretation and its conditions, the systematic reflection on all problems one could encounter when interpreting texts. It entailed a more fundamental mode of reflexivity that encompasses the very nature of the interpretative exercise, including the interpreter herself.

Hermeneutics assumes that the interpretative mode is fundamental to what makes us human (Malpas, 2015).[1]

For Schleiermacher and his romantic contemporaries like Friedrich Ast, Biblical texts were considered to express an unchanging human spirit. A text would lead to multiple *interpretations*, but this did not mean that its *meaning* was considered multiple as well. It was still assumed that there was one, singular meaning that did not change over time. The hermeneutic method therefore consisted of reconstructing that meaning, which entailed finding out the 'original' authorial intention. This meant an attempt to uncover the author's conscious *and* subconscious motivations, intentions, and associations. The ideal of the interpretative enterprise was therefore "[t]o know the author better than he knew himself," or: "to understand the text ... as well as and then even better than its author" (Schleiermacher, 1988, 124). An interpretation could never fully coincide with the text's meaning, so understanding could never be more than an approximation. Romantic hermeneutics emphasized imagination and feeling, in contrast and as a response to Enlightenment thought with its emphasis on logic.

An obstacle, here, was the fact that the text was created in a historical context that differed from the reader's lifeworld. An interpreter must bridge the temporal distance between the time of writing and reading, by placing the text back in original context and trying to fathom the way an author thought and perceived the world. One should verify sources—which edition is the correct one? How have the meanings of words changed? This meant looking at both form and content within the appropriate historical context. According to Schleiermacher, interpretation should affirm the internal coherence of a text, its unity of meaning. This meant that interpretation had to be closed off, and that the parts should be made fully coherent with the meaning of the whole. This maneuvering between part and whole has been referred to as the *hermeneutic circle*. This makes his approach to hermeneutics a 'restorative' or reconstructive one, as it tried to reconstruct the original meaning of the text in its own time. In sum, traditionally, hermeneutics employed a set of reconstruction techniques in a search for origins, for 'how it really was' (not unlike reconstructing a murder in a crime show). In modern hermeneutics, as will be discussed later, we still find this idea of the text as a symptom, with a secret hiding behind it.

The philosopher Martin Heidegger was the first to apply hermeneutics in a much broader sense than textual application. In his understanding, it came to be about no less than life itself. In his early work, Heidegger held that life is revealed in and through lived experiences [*Erlebnisse*]. Everything depends on our proper understanding of those experiences. What is encountered in them, is always already loaded with meaning. For Heidegger, understanding is therefore always rooted in a particular situation or opening toward the world, an ongoing "event" [*Ereignis*] in which we as humans participate. The experiencing self feels addressed by such an event and "ap-propriates" [*er-eignet*] it by making it part of its own self-understanding and life-story. So we are directly immersed in the world we live in, situated in life, without any form of mediation.

Heidegger did not believe that we are independent subjects who encounter distinct, not-yet interpreted objects outside their minds (the then-dominant view associated with Descartes). Instead, we know the world intimately. We do not hover above our objects of interpretation in a God-like and disembodied fashion, but are deeply connected to and familiar with the world. This direct and unmediated belonging-together of self and world, subject and object, puts hermeneutics at the center of everything we do. Hermeneutics, here, means investigating and clarifying our lived experiences. Because we are "thrown" into this world, our "factical life" always finds itself within a "handed-down, re-worked, or newly established interpretedness" (2005, 354),[2] we are always in a hermeneutic situation, in a particular interpretative space at a specific time. This space contains both past and present interpretations which we should critically assess and (re-)appropriate. Such a critical reflection allows for a better understanding of the self and the historical realities that inform its viewpoints.

In his magnum opus *Being and Time* (*Sein und Zeit*, 1927), Heidegger took this one step further. Here, he argues that humans are hermeneutic animals through and through. This means that understanding is not a conscious, intentional, and attentive procedure. In fact, Heidegger considered the most fundamental aspects of human existence in the world to be prescientific, and posited that we live surrounded by meanings passed on through tradition [*Überlieferung*, literally: the 'passing over' or 'handing down' of ideas and experiences]. Therefore, interpretation is essential for our survival, meaning that understanding is no less than *existence itself*. It stems from the interrelation between self, other, and world. Self-understanding and world-understanding thus presuppose each other. Heidegger's version of the hermeneutic circle is an ontological one. Here, understanding does not interpret a text: it interprets being itself. We see that with Heidegger, hermeneutics becomes much more than a methodological basis for the human sciences, or a mode of knowing to contrast objective explanation. It encompasses the 'event' of human existence as a whole, and as such is prior to all other modes of cognition and experience. It has even been said that with *Being and Time*, "philosophy itself becomes hermeneutic" (Hoy, 1993, 172). It is raised to the status of an *ontology* of human existence, a study of being itself.

Hans-Georg Gadamer was inspired by the 'ontological turn' of hermeneutics brought about by Heidegger, but applied it to textual interpretation. His most important addition to Heidegger's insights was that true understanding comes about through a dialogue between competing interpretations, guided by self-reflexivity, which could achieve a fusion of horizons. Where Dilthey and Schleiermacher sought meaning *behind* the text and searched for its origin, process of creation, and authorial intention, Gadamer, following up on Heidegger's ontology, searches for meaning *before* the text, in the space in-between text and reader. Like Schleiermacher, he starts from the insight that there is an "insuperable difference between the interpreter and the author" (2004, 296). But unlike the latter, he does not think 'reconstruction' is achievable. In *Truth and Method* (*Wahrheit und Methode*, 1960), Gadamer argues that textual meaning is dialogical, infinite, and infinitely changeable. Following Heidegger, he notes that the engagement with texts needs to be a fundamentally reflexive exercise. By interpreting a text, we enter into a dialogue, or productive "conversation" with it. In this process, we lay bare and question our own prejudices. In contrast to "the global demand of the Enlightenment" (Gadamer, 2004, 277) that all prejudice be left at the door when starting an analysis, Gadamer argues that "all understanding inevitably involves some prejudice [*Vorurteil*]" (272). These are the presuppositions, attitudes and experiences formed within a certain culture, that determine the world-vision of that culture. They pre-structure our seeing, hearing, feeling, and reading. The only way to draw our prejudices sharply into view, he suggested, is by letting them be provoked when a text addresses us in its strangeness or unintelligibility. He urges us to understand our prejudices as stemming from our deep involvement in, and convergence with the world, which are necessary for any act of understanding.

So how do we do this? In order to explain this, another important concept to add is that of the *horizon of interpretation*. Imagine an invisible wall of cultural and historical codes, traditions, and conventions that lies between interpreter and text. These determine our vision of the world without us even noticing, they form a filter for our interpretation. We are all trapped inside the horizon of our own time and culture and meanings are formed within this horizon. In contrast to Schleiermacher, Gadamer believed this horizon could not be transcended. At best, horizons could be brought together in a fusion, a convergence of vantage points of reader and text. This constitutes a rejection of both subjectivism and relativism; the locus of hermeneutics is a space of vacillation, an in-between (295). We are familiar with a text or artwork because it is 'handed down' to us, because it stands in a tradition, and yet its cultural or historical strangeness can never be suspended: "the circle of whole and part is not dissolved in perfect understanding but, on the contrary, is most fully realized" (293). What at first appears alien in the text can, upon close inspection, come to present a richer context of meaning. We gain a better and more profound understanding not only of the text but also of ourselves.

Importantly, Gadamer does not suggest we simply transpose ourselves into the horizon of the text. That would be more like an interview, a conversation in which one has only to get to know the other, without reciprocity. Instead, in a Gadamerian dialogue, both text or artwork and consciousness are implicated. It is this search for commonality, understood as a recognition in the face of strangeness, of which Gadamer said:

> Hermeneutics must start from the position that a person seeking to understand something has a bond to the subject matter that comes into language

through the traditionary text and has, or acquires, a connection with the tradition from which the text speaks.

(295)

That is, understanding the tradition from which a text or artwork speaks is no precondition to its total understanding. The further the distance between interpreter and artwork, the more space for tradition to unfurl. Temporal distance thus becomes a productive condition for understanding. "It is not a yawning abyss but is filled with the continuity of custom and tradition, in the light of which everything handed down presents itself to us" (297). For Gadamer, understanding operates by way of the 'fore-structures' of understanding, involving the fore-conception of completeness [*der Vorgriff der Vollkommenheit*]. This is the (provisional) presupposition that the text or object to be understood is essentially understandable, since it is a coherent and therefore meaningful whole. Truly understanding a text and gaining insight in this way is an event, it happens partly beyond our control. Interpretation is therefore partly subjective but not relativist (or 'anything goes)': it is intersubjective. It asks for an openness on the part of the interpreter, who has to allow herself to be changed by the text or object they are is interpreting. The dialogical fusion of horizons renders the familiar (our own horizon, codes, traditions) strange. In sum, Gadamer's dialogism precisely foregrounds the difference, the gap between interpreter and other. This entails making the self, the familiar, strange, as much as familiarizing oneself with the other's viewpoint.

Hermeneutics, and especially Gadamer's dialogical approach, inspired theorists of race and ethnicity as well as sex and gender in his insistence on the cultural situatedness of the self. The notion of a horizon from which meanings are formed in a particular culture and time turned out to be particularly fruitful for such theories. Gadamer's hermeneutics accounts for a social reality that allows women-centered research to make claims to legitimacy, while feminist theory adds new social and political angles (Buker, 1990). But Gadamer's hermeneutics has also been criticized for not sufficiently accounting for the effects of power (see for instance Code, 2003).

Feminist standpoint theory, or standpoint epistemology, can be considered hermeneutic while emphasizing unequal power distributions. It tries to epistemically valorize the more discredited or marginalized knowledge perspectives. It focuses on the social construction of the category "women" as a subject of study and source of knowledge that is rooted in women's experiences. Susan Harding (1996) argues that, if we discard the notion that knowing is universal and accept that all knowing will significantly imply the standpoint, or socio-historical situatedness, of specific knowers, this will only increase our capacity to achieve objectivity. Scientific methods often do not analyze the context in which discovery takes place, including all kinds of social desires, interests, and values that shape science. This makes it look like science is without a subject, a disembodied reporting of value-free, context-independent facts. However, Harding writes, science does have a subject (usually male) with a standpoint, a perspective that involves assumptions and values based on activities of this dominant group. When the dominant group is homogeneous, its standpoint is epistemically limited with respect to that of more marginalized groups. To counteract this, Harding promotes standpoint epistemology as a methodology that involves "starting off thought from the lives of marginalized peoples" (1996, 445). This would reveal the unexamined assumptions that inform science and generate critical inquiries, paradoxically amounting more objective (because less partial and distorted) accounts.

In *Epistemic Injustice: Power and the Ethics of Knowing*, Miranda Fricker adds to standpoint epistemology the notion of "hermeneutical injustice": "The injustice of having some significant area of one's social experience obscured from collective understanding owing to a structural identity prejudice in the collective hermeneutical resource" (Fricker, 2007, 155). Fricker postulates that in any culture and time, a "collective hermeneutical resource" is at work. This resource, not unlike a Gadamerian horizon, contains the tools that help us understand our experiences. When the tools to process an experience are missing, this experience is left out of the epistemic framework of a culture. Before the #metoo movement, for instance, there was no good way for a victim of some of the more 'grey areas' of harassment and power abuse to understand and vocalize what had happened to them, simply because the collective hermeneutical resource was incomplete. When groups are being excluded from the generation of collective understanding, Fricker calls this hermeneutical marginalization. We will explore the concept at more length in Chapter 4.

Against/Beyond Interpretation?

Not every scholar, however, is enthusiastic about the prevalence of hermeneutic notions and practices in the study of literature and culture. This has to do with the fact that in practice, as stated in the beginning of this chapter, hermeneutics often meant looking for double layers, beyond the literal, for meanings that are invisible at first glance. Since Homeric times, literature has been *allegorical*, which literally means 'saying something different': words do not mean what they say. Greek Homeric Allegory, Christian exegesis of the Bible, and Dante's four levels of interpretation, but also modern hermeneutics, all have this in common: they look for hidden meanings (Brillenburg Wurth, 2018). Susan Sontag traces this tendency back to Plato's and Aristotle's mimetic theories of art. Both philosophers understood mimesis (which translates to imitation, representation and emulation) as the representation of nature. Think of Plato's cave allegory, where the people can only see shades of the objects in the real world. This parallels our empirical reality, where according to Plato we only see the objects in the world, mere reflections of the realm of Ideas. For Plato, truth did not lie in what was directly available to the senses. Sontag also mentions the Gnostic tradition from the second century in this respect, where valued knowledge should remain veiled and secret, unspoken and unspeakable.

According to Sontag, since then, art has always dominantly been seen as representation of reality. This idea leads critics to (artificially) separate something called form, from something called content: an act which Sontag calls interpretation. Art needs to be justified; it cannot exist on its own. In the Enlightenment, for instance, marked by a shift from a mythic to realistic worldview, the ancient texts, full of religious symbols, had to be adapted to the world of contemporary readers. The Stoics posed that the gods were moral creatures, so their uncivilized behavior in Homer's epic had to be interpreted allegorically to make this fit. They proposed that Zeus' adultery with Leto *really* stood for the union between power and wisdom, in a typical move of interpretation: "X is *really* Y." Interpretation presents an incongruity between the text and the demands of its (later) readers and tries to dissolve it.

Even though this take on interpretation is as old as Antiquity, it saw its heyday in the 1970s and 1980s, when many scholarly disciplines in the Humanities and social sciences became influenced by Marxism and psychoanalysis as "metalanguages." Sigmund Freud, in his *Traumdeutung* (1900), interpreted dreams and the unconscious by separating manifest from latent content. Marx interpreted social reality by looking for deeper layers, like substructure versus superstructure. In both cases, a subtext is sought, as it were, 'behind' the text, which is what it 'really' means. This led to an approach to textual interpretation that understood meaning to be "hidden, repressed, deep, and in need of detection and disclosure by an interpreter" (Best & Marcus, 2009, 1), which is often called symptomatic reading. It holds that the truest meaning of a text or other cultural product lies in what it *does not* say.

Paul Ricoeur famously identified two basic tenets of doing hermeneutics in this respect, which will play a central role in the book you are reading: the hermeneutics of faith and of suspicion (or distrust). The hermeneutics of distrust, among which Ricoeur counts the work of Freud, Marx, Nietzsche, and Foucault, reads a text for what it does not say, a repressed or hidden message. The hermeneutics of faith, or trust, is exemplified by Bible exegesis and the phenomenology of religion, where meaning is not understood to lie at the surface can only unfold when it reveals its profound truth to an interpreter who is able to disclose it, often by reading between the lines. Meaning is considered as disguised and distorted, but the interpreter does not try to subvert it in a hostile manner. They stand in awe with respect to the strange text, feeling themselves addressed it and respectfully tries to unveil its meaning. Rita Felski calls these, respectively, "ideological" and "theological" styles of criticism: either reducing texts to political instruments or revering in their sheer ineffability (2015, 29). According to Ricoeur, they are both necessary, but critics like Felski and Sontag have expressed their discontent with such styles of hermeneutics that take a text to mean something beyond the text and look for secret double layers.

The last decades have witnessed a surge of books, articles, and movements that pronounce post- or anti-hermeneutic times and propose approaches that go 'beyond' interpretation—from media archaeology (Kittler, 1999) to object-oriented ontology (Harman, 2002) and speculative realism (Meillassoux, 2008) and from 'thin description' (Love, 2010; 2013) to 'surface reading' (Best & Marcus, 2009) and 'reparative reading' (Sedgwick, 2003). Some speak of the 'material turn' in the Humanities and social sciences, others of a 'turn away from the linguistic turn'[3] (Brillenburg Wurth, 2018; Orlemanski, 2014). Such ideas and approaches, some of which will be revisited in Chapter 3, often advocate attention to affect, matter, forms, non-human entities, description, and surfaces. We will not dwell on them here, but Julie Orlemanski helpfully summarizes that these anti-hermeneutic orientations toward reading (alternatively called 'anti-critical' or 'anti-correlationist') go against some of the main properties of hermeneutic thought: "depth, consciousness, the primacy of language, humanism, interpretation, mediation, epistemology, and historicism" (226). They call upon readers to change their attitudes toward the text (less 'paranoid,' more accepting or even loving).

But when we look around us, it is clear to see that, despite these critical efforts, hermeneutics is not dead. Rather than alleging that we are living in post-hermeneutic times, we argue that hermeneutics has become ever more pervasive, if in less centralized ways. It has migrated from a range of philosophical theories and approaches in literary studies, to prevalent practices in online culture at large that warrant scholarly reflection. In this book, we discuss a range of such practices of hermeneutics 'in the wild' in digital culture. We are all hermeneuts. Beyond academia, we will see, a deeply hermeneutic attitude characterizes our engagement with connective media. Internet platforms abound with fan communities, subcultures, and conspiracy theorists who view the world as full of hidden meaning waiting to be revealed. Time and again, a 'real,' more true reality is presupposed that lies behind the appearances of cultural expressions, which need to be decoded in order for the truth to be revealed. Scholars of literature and culture, whose training remains steeped in the hermeneutic tradition (whether we like it or not) have the theoretical and critical tools at our disposal to recognize, respond to, and engage with the age-old problems of interpretation and suspicion that have come to dominate public life online.

A Hermeneutics for Online Culture?

To update and revamp the hermeneutic tradition and come to an approach to studying online culture that would help address problems related to trust, distrust, and polarization that we started with, we must connect the hermeneutic tradition to the digital humanities: the field that combines traditional humanities with digital technology. What would a digital or online version of hermeneutics look like? There is work to do before the two can be brought together. In fact, the rise of digital humanities has sometimes been seen as part of the anti-hermeneutic turn in the humanities over the past decades that we briefly outlined. After all, working with 'objective' data rather than necessarily having to read texts might (misleadingly!) suggest that the need for interpretation is somewhat lessened, that we can just let the data speak for themselves. Hermeneutics, as the tradition of interpretation that emphasizes the always already mediated character of meaning, which necessitates 'decoding,' might seem alien or at best marginal to this semi-objective collection of methods, a thing of the past.

Text mining, machine-reading, algorithmic analyses and other digital humanities methods help us navigate the problems of the information age, often described as 'too many books, too little time.' As whole libraries have by now been digitized, an issue arises that Matthew Wilkens has called the "problem of abundance":

> We don't read any faster than we ever did, even as the quantity of text produced grows larger by the year. If we need to read books in order to extract information from them and if we need to have read things in common in order to talk about them, we're going to spend most of our time dealing with a relatively small set of texts ... each of us reads only a truly minuscule fraction of contemporary fiction (on the order of 0.1 percent, often much less). ... we need to decide what to ignore.
>
> (2011, 250)

One solution to the problem of abundance is 'distant reading,' the practice of aggregating and processing information about, or content in, large bodies of texts without the necessity of a human reader who reads these texts. "Reading" is outsourced to a computer. Distant reading is a form of data mining that allows information in (e.g., subjects, places, actors) or about (e.g., author, title, date, number of pages) the text to be processed and analyzed. The latter are called metadata: data about data. Natural Language Processing (NLP) can summarize the contents of 'unreadably' large corpora of texts, while with data mining, we can expose patterns on scales beyond human hermeneutic capacity. Franco Moretti, founder of the Stanford Literary Lab, introduced the term in explicit opposition to close reading, which, to his mind, fails to uncover the true scope of literature: "[D]istance ... is a condition of knowledge: it allows you to perceive patterns and to focus on units that are much smaller or much larger than the text: devices, themes, tropes — or genres and systems" (Moretti, 2000, 57). This is coming from a place of distrust in close reading, which is necessarily selective and therefore prone to bias. Digital humanists seek to address this by separating (scientific and data-driven) methodology from acts of interpretation. Best and Marcus (2009) imagine that digital humanities introduces a form of analysis that *bypasses subjectivity*:

> Where the heroic critic corrects the text, a nonheroic critic might aim instead to correct for her critical subjectivity, by using machines to bypass

it, in the hopes that doing so will produce more accurate knowledge about texts.

(2009, 17)

They seem to believe the algorithm can produce this "accurate knowledge" without being situated in a world with cultural knowledge, bias, and ideology. Since algorithms cannot view the text in terms of hidden depth, Best and Marcus expect digital humanities approaches to bring in "objectivity, validity, truth" (17), which had long been "taboo" in the Humanities. Likewise, scholars in Computational Literary Studies, like Andrew Piper (2016), claim that literary critics no longer have to make unsupported claims about periods in literary history, based on only a limited number of texts. CLS offers a way to support claims and go against previously unchecked 'received wisdom' using empirical evidence.

Katherine Bode criticizes Moretti and some of his peers, like Matthew Jockers, for perceiving data and computation as offering full and unmediated access to literary history, thereby disregarding the interpretive activities that go into making the data and the digital record available in the first place. She writes that these digital humanities scholars consistently present literary data as facts, rather than interpretations. Moretti seems to envision data visualization as a "transparent window onto history" (Bode, 2018, 20), while Jockers has written that any "leap from the specific to the general" is flawed because it is based on interpretation (Jockers, 2013, 28). Orlemanski even claims that, by trying to side-step close or human reading, Moretti loses the "recursive oscillation between text and context, form and history. In other words, he steps out of the hermeneutic circle" (223).

Clearly, such ideas about sidestepping acts of interpretation are misguided when it comes to the study of culture. José van Dijck (2014) warns us not to assume that, through data, which in Latin means "given," in the sense of "fact," the "real" is transmitted, as if independent of representation and the subjective human perspective. Data is by no means "free" from human subjectivity, just because it is quantitative: every data point is an abstraction, and every dataset is selected and created by humans according to human criteria (Dobson, 2015). Data are thus already the result of interpretive choices, and curated datasets are necessarily selective (Da, 2019). As we clearly see in these critiques, hermeneutic concerns have never been off the table, even in digital humanities and digital literary studies. But would it be possible to use computational methods in the service of hermeneutics?

The answer is yes, and it has been done. Here, we briefly look at several attempts to integrate close and distant reading approaches and develop methods of reading on different scales, as well as a number of existing theories for a 'digital hermeneutics,' before outlining our own approach in this book. The subdiscipline of Critical Code Studies (Marino, 2020) unravels layers of meaning in computer source code as a semiotic, material, cultural, and social text. As such, it can be seen as a hermeneutic approach where the human center partly gives way to the machinic, or rather: to a dialogue between programmer, machine, and recipient. Computer code, after all, is hidden beneath the surface of the texts we see. As Rita Raley argues, "Code may in a general sense be opaque and legible only to specialists, much like a cave painting's sign system, but it has been inscribed, programmed, written. It is conditioned and concretely historical" (2006, par. 28). Often, the hermeneutics of code are of the suspicious type, for instance, where Mark Marino signals "a growing sense that the code we are not reading is working against our interests" (2020, 3).

Dennis Tenen, in *Plain Text: The Poetics of Computation* (2017), likewise reflects on the nature of 'digital inscription.' He argues that today, readers and interpreters are in a position of "selective asemiosis," or loss of signification, caused by the pervasiveness of objects that are not accessible for us to read with the human senses and brain, like encrypted software. This necessitates studying mechanisms of codification, if we wish to remain capable of critique. Tenen therefore proposes to couple critical theory with computer science and engineering, which he calls computational poetics: "a strategy of interpretation capable of reaching past surface content to reveal platforms and infrastructures that stage the construction of meaning" (6).

Algorithmic parameters are set by humans, meaning that human biases and prejudices can come to be programmed within the algorithm itself. Algorithmic bias refers to how negative biases against minority groups can come to be embedded in technical infrastructure. In *Algorithms of Oppression*, Safiya Umoja Noble shows how discrimination is embedded in code and AI technologies. She analyzes algorithms as 'redlining': automated digital decision-making systems that strengthen social relationships of oppression and perform new modes of racial profiling. By reminding us that even mathematical formulations are created by human beings and thus perpetuate and reinforce the biases in culture, we could say, Noble implicitly makes a case for a hermeneutics of algorithms.

In addition, several authors have reflected in a more explicit way on the use of hermeneutics for understanding how digital technologies mediate between human beings and the world.[4] Paolo Gerbaudo (2016) proposes a 'data hermeneutics' to counteract the ideology of dataism, emphasizing the need for sampling or selection procedures in digital humanities methodologies, rather than automatized pattern detection on a macro-scale. To this end, he advocates qualitative sampling procedures to reduce the size of datasets, and a mode of analysis that he calls data close readings. His method consists of reading posts first as rows in a dataset, then as part of a dialogue, and last as part of a social discourse.

Rafael Capurro also writes about 'digital hermeneutics,' to denote a hermeneutics that engages with the challenges offered by digital technology, an "understanding [of] the foundations of digital technology and its interplay with human existence" (2010, 37). He diagnoses the 'weakening' of modern technology in two different senses: there is a weakening of the interpreter who finds herself within a network of human and nonhuman actants that she cannot really control. In addition, he calls information technology itself a weak technology, as it necessarily puts human language and conversations central. For Capurro, this attests to the deep entanglement between the digital and hermeneutics. The former questions the interpreter's autonomy, while the latter could be capable of analyzing and eventually reconfiguring the structure of the technological system. From an anthropological perspective, he concludes, digital hermeneutics questions our interpretational autonomy as human beings, the loss of control over the way we interpret the world, induced by technology.

For Alberto Romele (2020), who is inspired by Don Ihde, digital technologies themselves are hermeneutic. By this, he means that they present us with representations of the world that we must interpret in order to have access to the world. In this respect, he also stresses the need to distinguish between the interpretative agencies of humans and those of non-human actors. Digital technologies are capable of "minimizing the distance between the world and its representations" (18) which means that they run the risk of reducing the world to its technological representations. Romele also criticizes the way that hermeneutics traditionally tends to favor language, ignoring the materiality of technological mediators in transmitting meaning. Romele et al. (2018) envision digital hermeneutics as an emerging discipline and set of methodological issues, insisting that "dealing with digital methods and digital objects for approaching specific entities such as political opinion is still a form of interpretation, no matter how automated and quantified these methods are" (4). Rather than ending this chapter with a conclusion like we will do with the others, we will conclude by outlining our own approach to digital hermeneutics that will be used in the chapters to come.

Scaled Reading: Reconfiguring the Hermeneutic Circle

In this book, we present a range of pedagogical strategies for the interpretation of online culture to tackle the urgent challenges of trust and distrust in the information age. Our approach to a hermeneutics of digital culture builds on a method previously set out by Tom van Nuenen and Inge van de Ven in previous publications (Van Nuenen & van de Ven, 2020; Van de Ven & Van Nuenen, 2022) and developed and used in several educational settings. In the face of sentiments described, including the increasing weight in Western culture of doubt, skepticism, and the overvaluing of independent truth-finding, and inspired by the dialogical hermeneutics set out by Gadamer in *Truth and Method*, we stress the importance of interpretation as a dialogical process. Updating the hermeneutic circle for digital humanities, our approach combines reading strategies and computational tools and methods to analyze online corpora in a circular structure or feedback loop that vacillates between the big data ('N=all') perspective of the whole, and a close reading of the part or the sample. Thus, we reconfigure the hermeneutic circle, which traditionally alternates attention from part to whole and back, as a circle from distant to close reading and back. The scaled readings we perform in the following three chapters, do not just oscillate between 'distant' and 'close,' but also build epistemological bridges between the familiar and the strange. This way, digital literary and cultural studies should help students understand how different horizons structure the world differently, opposing the idea of a singular truth or 'correct' worldview (and concurrent polarization).

To this end, interpretation and method should not be envisioned as separate steps. Without denying its relevance, Gadamer, inspired by Heidegger, emphasized the limited role of method in hermeneutics, understood as a set of rules. As noted, he conceived of understanding as an ongoing, always incomplete process, in which truth is an event of disclosure in which the interpreter is already involved. Because of its event-like character that happens partly beyond the control of the interpreter, no method could render this process fully transparent. In response, Ricoeur later nuanced what he saw as too sharp an opposition between truth and method in Gadamer. For him, they were equally important and went hand in glove, hence his adage, to "explain more in order to understand better" (2000, 125). In the case of our scaled readings, the zooming in on a dataset from larger-scale data to a sample for close reading can be seen as a method, where we see the event-like nature of interpretation unfold at every level or scale. Although we use tools and data-centered methods like topic modeling on some of these levels, which could be viewed as explication rather than interpretation, method and interpretation are integrated at every scale. Indeed, rather than constituting separate steps, truth and method, interpretation and data, and the familiar and the strange should be seen as closely entangled in this approach.

Our method is part description, part intervention. At the descriptive level, we show that hermeneutics is 'what people do' in online communities on a grand scale. We add a layer of scrutiny to that, an intervention that lays bare the complexities of the application and adaptation of hermeneutics to the digital. Our readings of a number of visual-textual case studies from contemporary online culture draw out the complexities inherent in adapting hermeneutics to the digital, and they are repeatable for a variety of online contexts (some suggestions for further application are offered in Chapter 5). We 'read' cultural objects (like discussion threads and memes) on the following five levels or 'scales,' which we elaborate in the following chapters. For some of these, we use tools for performing natural language processing (NLP). NLP uses computers to process text and to aid in the identification of meaningful subjects and discursive patterns in unstructured textual data.

1 *Platform hermeneutics* entails an examination of the specific affordances of the respective platforms, and how they relate to specific modes of self-expression and anonymity.

2 *Contextual reading* involves an examination of the contextual horizon against which we can understand the (visual or linguistic) particularity of the respective corpora.
3 *Distant reading* offers insight into the most important themes and semantic fields for each corpus.
4 *Hyper-reading* traces patterns of discursive particularities and themes back to their original context in the corpus.
5 *Close reading* is a way to look at inherent and internal tensions, conflicts, and irony that may have been found on the previous scales, and to examine the stylistic features of the discourse.

The overall oscillation, ranging from platform hermeneutics to distant reading to a close reading of individual posts, could lead to a new iteration of the cycle. We will demonstrate this approach in Chapters 2–4, focusing on different scales and methods dependent on the case study. The scaled readings will be applied to three case studies in digital culture: depression memes on online platforms, the 2022 Johnny Depp/Amber Heard defamation trial, and the subreddit r/changemyview. In our concluding chapter, we propose three additional case studies to use in educational settings. As online environments make it neither possible nor desirable to separate the textual from the visual, we make a case for the inclusion of the visual. Moreover, we specifically rethink hermeneutic theory in the context of online platforms and the ways in which they afford and limit human experience.

In the process, it is also necessary to problematize any straightforward application of text-centered hermeneutic approaches to these new technological infrastructures and interfaces that radically transform the ways in which humans make sense of cultural expressions. Here, we take cue from Ihde who, with his post-phenomenology or 'material hermeneutics' set out in *Technology and the Lifeworld* (1990), argues that human access to the world is always already mediated, which makes technologies hermeneutic "by nature." Mediating between humans and world, they magnify certain aspects of it and reduce others. Technologies are selective, they do not simply replicate non-technological situations, and they are 'multistable,' meaning they have different uses and effects in different social and cultural contexts. What Ihde considers "hermeneutic" is a specific kind of technologically mediated human-world relation, where the technology offers a representation of the world that must be 'interpreted' to access the world. This opens up hermeneutics to non-human entities. The question becomes, how interpretational agency is distributed between humans and machines.

How does this distribution of agency work in the case of algorithms that are said to do the work of interpretation for us? An often-cited online article opens with:

Can algorithms interpret the works of Shakespeare in depth? Yes, they can, and they do it with a precision that many literature professors could only dream to achieve. Do they understand where the authentic value of paint-ings by renowned artists lies? Absolutely!

(Biedrzycki, 2021)

Such jubilant statements can only be considered true if we have a very idi-osyncratic understanding of 'interpretation' and 'understanding': one that is in fact closer to explication than to hermeneutics. AI is good at pattern rec-ognition: when 'analyzing' paintings, for instance, it can distinguish between different sorts of brush strokes, and thereby authenticate to some extent who the creator was, often better than humans can. It is important to note, how-ever, that this is not an act of understanding. Then, there are projects like ArtEmis, which "teach" algorithms to "interpret" emotional responses to art (Myers, 2021). However useful, this is not truly understanding the artwork either: it is automatically identifying, detecting, and being able to reproduce a range of human responses to art. Understanding (unlike explication) can-not be seen apart from participating in life (Dilthey, 1966). For Gadamer and Ricoeur, we deeply belong to the world we interpret: "Life interprets itself. Life itself has a hermeneutical structure" (Gadamer, 2004, 221). Although technologies like algorithms are increasingly part of our lives, they lack the "lived experience" (Dilthey, 1997) at the basis of understanding. Therefore, hermeneutically speaking, technology does not 'understand' as such, at best explain (Gransche, 2018).

So do algorithms themselves have interpretive agency? As will be dis-cussed in Chapter 3, people certainly project onto algorithms the agency to interpret for them, for example when they experience personalized content as revealing something profound about themselves. Algorithms have the ability to make automated decisions, but they are not autonomous: as technologies, they are non-neutral and structurally ambiguous (Ihde, 1990, 144). They are rules that sort and correlate data, developed and programmed by humans with human values and ideologies. Insofar as they can be said to have agency at all, it is thus shaped by humans and institutions. Programmers and software engineers deliver input in the form of relevant criteria and instructions and pre-select possible outcomes (Klinger & Svensson, 2018, 4654). The cal-culations thus programmed are shaped by data; the output is based on the agency embedded in earlier steps and in need to be interpreted again by hu-mans (Gransche, 2018). Whereas human agency is situated and emergent (it develops as we confront new situations), algorithms evaluate the past and pro-ject the future based on past behaviors, but cannot yet transform themselves beyond their design, since they lack reflexivity (Klinger & Svensson, 2018). This means that algorithms cannot do the work of interpretation for us.

And yet, from the perspective of Ihde's (1990) post-phenomenology, technologies can be considered hermeneutic in a broader sense of mediat-ing between humans and the world. Hermeneutics *is* this technologically mediated human-world relation, including the representations of the world that technology presents to us. Interpretational agency is distributed between humans and non-human, machinic others. Even though algorithms on their own lack reflexive and interpretative agency, we can thus understand algorithmic processes as techno-hermeneutic assemblages which include interpretation at several stages. In what follows, we will understand platforms as such techno-hermeneutic assemblages and include them in our hermeneutic inquiries. A platform-specific approach allows us to see the internet as disseminated into different spaces where rules for interpretation vary according to infrastructural and cultural grammars. Each platform constructs new ways to read, with their own set of deliberative parameters technologically imposed through affordances. Therefore, ways to deliberate, and ways to read deliberation, proliferate. In what follows, we will look at examples of the ways that deliberation differs in different case analyses, while situating them in a multi-platform ecosystem.

Notes

1 Friedrich Nietzsche even famously stated that everything is interpretation, and everything (including the text itself) is an interpreter. The world, nature and, in fact, the whole cosmos was "hermeneutic" through and through for Nietzsche (Babich, 2015).
2 Translation in Farin (2015).
3 With "turn away from the linguistic turn," Orlemanski refers to the "acknowledged disintegration of the analogy between linguistic science, literary reading, and social analysis" (2014, 224).
4 For a more comprehensive overview of such approaches, see Romele (2020); Van Nuenen and Van de Ven (2022).

References

Babich, B. (2014). Nietzsche and the Ubiquity of Hermeneutics. In Malpas, J., & Gander, H. H. (Eds.), *The Routledge Companion to Hermeneutics* (pp. 85–97). London and New York: Routledge.

Best, S., & Marcus, S. (2009). Surface Reading: An Introduction. *Representations*, 108, 1–21.

Biedrzycki, N. (2021, July 13). Machine Learning. A Literature Expert and Art Connoisseur. https://norbertbiedrzycki.pl/en/machine-learning-a-literature-expert-and-an-art-connoisseur

Bode, K. (2018). *A World of Fiction: Digital Collections and the Future of Literary History.* University of Michigan Press.

Brillenburg Wurth, K. (2018). The Material Turn in Comparative Literature: An Introduction. *Comparative Literature*, 70(3), 247–263.

Buker, E. A. (1990). Feminist Social Theory and Hermeneutics: An Empowering Dialectic? *Social Epistemology*, 4(1), 23–39.

Capurro, R. (2010). Digital Hermeneutics: An Outline. *AI and Society*, 25, 35–42. DOI: 10.1007/s00146-009-0255-9

Chin, C. (2019, April 6). Change My View' Reddit Community Launches Its Own Website. *Wired.* https://www.wired.com/story/change-my-view-gets-its-own-website/

Code, L. (Ed.) (2003). *Feminist Interpretations of Hans-Georg Gadamer*. Philadephia, PA: Pennsylvania State University Press.

Da, N. Z. (2019). The Computational Case against Computational Literary Studies. *Critical Inquiry*, 45(3), 601–639.

Dilthey, W. (1966). *Gesammelte schriften (1914–2005)*. Göttingen: Vandenhoeck & Ruprecht.

Dobson, J. E. (2015). Can an Algorithm Be Disturbed? Machine Learning, Intrinsic Criticism, and the Digital Humanities. *College Literature: A Journal of Critical Literary Studies*, 42(4), 543–564.

van Dijck, J. (2014). Datafication, Dataism and Dataveillance: Big Data between Scientific Paradigm and Ideology. *Surveillance & Society*, 12(2), 197–208.

Farin, I. (2015). Heidegger: Transformation of Hermeneutics. In Malpas, J., & Gander, H. H. (Eds.), *The Routledge Companion to Hermeneutics* (pp. 149–159). London and New York: Routledge.

Felski, R. (2015). *The Limits of Critique*. Chicago, IL: The University of Chicago Press.

Fricker, M. (2007). *Epistemic Injustice: Power and the Ethics of Knowing*. Oxford: Oxford University Press.

Gadamer, H. G. (2004). *Truth and Method*, 2nd ed. Trans. D. G. Marshall. London & New York: Continuum.

Gerbaudo, P. (2016). From Data Analytics to Data Hermeneutics: The Continuing Relevance of Interpretive Approaches. *Digital Culture and Society*, 2(2), 95–112. DOI: 10.14361/DCS-2016-0207

Gransche, B. (2018). Free the Text! The Texture-Turn in the Philosophy of Technology. In Reijers, W., Romele, A., & Coeckelberg, M. (Eds.), *Interpreting Technology: Ricoeur on Questions Concerning Ethics and Philosophy of Technology* (pp. 75–96). Lanham, MD: Rowman & Littlefield.

Harding, S. (1996). Gendered Ways of Knowing and the "Epistemological Crisis" of the West. In Goldberger, N. R. (Eds.), *Knowledge, Difference, and Power: Essays Inspired by Women's Ways of Knowing*, 1st ed (pp. 431–454). New York, NY: Basic Books.

Harman, G. (2002). *Tool-Being: Heidegger and the Metaphysics of Objects*. Peru, IL: Open Court.

Heidegger, M. (2010). *Being and Time*. Trans. Macquarrie, J. New York, NY: State University of New York Press.

Heidegger, M. (2005). *Phänomenologische Interpretationen Ausgewählter Abhandlungen Des Aristoteles Zur Ontologie Und Logik, Gesamtausgabe, Vol. 62*. Frankfurt am Main: Vittorio Klostermann.

Hoy, D. C. (1993). Heidegger and the Hermeneutic Turn. In Guignon, C. (Ed.), *The Cambridge Companion to Heidegger* (pp. 170–194). Cambridge, UK: Cambridge University Press.

Ihde, D. (1990). *Technology and the Lifeworld*. Bloomington, IN: Indiana University Press.

Jockers, M. (2013). *Macroanalysis: Digital Methods and Literary History*. Champaign, IL: University of Illinois Press.

Kittler, F. (1999). *Gramophone, Film, Typewriter* (G. Winthrop-Young, & M. Wutz Trans). Stanford, CA: Stanford University Press.

Klinger, U., & Svensson, J. (2018). The End of Media Logics? On Algorithms and Agency. *New Media & Society*, 20(12), 4653–4670. DOI: 10.1177/1461444818779750

Love, H. (2013). *Close Reading and Thin Description*. Durham, NC: Duke University Press.

Love, H. (2010). Close but not Deep: Literary Ethics and the Descriptive Turn. *New Literary History*, 41, 371–391.

Marino, M. (2020). *Critical Code Studies*. Cambridge, MA: The MIT Press.

Meillassoux, Q. (2008). *After Finitude*. Edinburgh: A&C Black.

Moretti, F. (2000). Conjectures on World Literature. *New Left Review*, 2(1), 54–68.

Myers, A. (2021, March 22). Artist's Intent: AI Recognizes Emotions in Visual Art. https://hai.stanford.edu/news/artists-intent-ai-recognizes-emotions-visual-art

Van Nuenen, T., & Van de Ven, I. (2020). Digital Hermeneutics and Media Literacy: Teaching the Red Pill across Horizons. *Tilburg Papers in Culture Studies*, paper 241.

Noble, S. U. (2018). *Algorithms of Oppression. How Search Engines Reinforce Racism*. New York: New York University Press.

Orlemanski, J. (2014). Scales of Reading. *Exemplaria: Medieval, Early Modern, Theory*, 26(2–3), 215–233.

Piper, A. (2016). There Will Be Numbers. *Journal of Cultural Analytics*, 1(1), 1–10.

Raley, R. (2006). Code.surface| |Code.depth. In *Dichtung Digital. Journal für Kunst und Kultur digitaler Medien* 36(8), 1–24. DOI: 10.25969/mediarep/17695

Ricoeur, P. (1970). *Freud and Philosophy: An Essay on Interpretation* (D. Savage Trans). New Haven, CT: Yale University Press.

Ricoeur, P. (1976). *Interpretation Theory: Discourse and the Surplus of Meaning*. Fort Worth: Texas Christian University Press.

Ricoeur, P. (2007). *The Conflict of Interpretations. Essays in Hermeneutics*. Evanston, IL: Northwestern University Press.

Ricoeur, P. (2000). *The Just* (D. Pellauer Trans). Chiacgo, IL: The University of Chicago Press.

Romele, A. (2020). *Digital Hermeneutics: Philosophical Investigations in New Media and Technology*. London and New York: Routledge.

Romele, A., Severo, M., & Furia, P. (2018). Digital Hermeneutics: From Interpreting with Machines to Interpretational Machines. In *AI and Society: Knowledge, Culture and Communication* 35(1), 73–86.

Schleiermacher, F. (1988). *Schleiermacher: Hermeneutics and Criticism And Other Writings* (Eds. Bowie, A., & Clarke, D. M.). Cambridge: Cambridge University Press.

Sedgwick, E. K. (2003). *Touching Feeling: Affect, Pedagogy, Performativity*. Durham, NC: Duke University Press.

Sontag, S. (2001 [1966]). *Against Interpretation and Other Essays*. New York: Farrar, Straus & Giroux. 3–14.

Tenen, D. (2017). *Plain Text: The Poetics of Computation*. Standford, CA: Stanford University Press.

Tripodi, F. (2018). Alternative Facts, Alternative Truths. *Medium*, February 23. https://points.datasociety.net/alternative-facts-alternative-truths-ab9d446b06c

Van de Ven, I., & Van Nuenen, T. (2022). Digital Hermeneutics: Scaled Readings of Online Depression Discourses. *Medical Humanities*, 48(3), 335–346. DOI: 10.1136/medhum-2020-012104

Wilkens, M. (2011). Canons, Close Reading, and the Evolution of Method. In Matthew K. Gold (Ed.), *Debates in the Digital Humanities* (pp. 249–258). Minneapolis: University of Minnesota Press.

2 Paranoid Readings of Toxic Memes

Suspicious Hermeneutics

The Small Things Hardly Noticeable

After the world-famous pop singer Britney Spears suffered a mental health crisis, she was placed under legal conservatorship of her father in 2008, a situation that would last for 13 years. Some of her fans, convinced that Spears is being held prisoner and is sending her fans secret messages through her social media, founded the #FreeBritney movement,. They started to parse her Instagram account for hidden messages, for instance by scrutinizing the singer's choice of clothes. When she wore yellow, this was interpreted as signifying "danger." When Spears posted a picture of a decaying rose with the caption: "If you will stay close to nature... to its simplicity... to the small things hardly noticeable... those things can unexpectedly become great and immeasurable," this immediately triggered epistemic vigilance: "It sounds like a clue. Like to look for the small things in her posts like the things not noticeable"; "[t]he rose doesn't look too great... maybe a sign?". Even a year after her conservatorship ended and Spears should effectively have been freed, her most active fans spend around 30 hours per week investigating. Fans inspect her viral videos frame by frame and point at glitches, lags, and photoshop mistakes and create TikTok videos with titles like "Proof Britney Spears Was Replaced by an A.I. on Her Wedding Day."

This chapter engages with the hermeneutics of suspicion, a mode of interpretation rooted in post-Enlightenment philosophies that started to subject the idea of reason, or consciousness itself, to critical inquiry. It holds that meaning is distorted and the task of the interpreter is to unmask, demystify, and reduce illusions. We argue that today, this mode of interpretation has given rise to paranoid reading practices that are widespread beyond academia. Among certain demographics, we see a decrease in trust when it comes to former sources of authority such as journalistic media, scientists, and experts. Political polarization and the mainstreaming of conspiracy thought has led to a deep-seated distrust of groups outside of their own community and of things as they seem. In Europe and the United States, trust in the media has been steadily eroding since the 1960s (Bialik & Matsa, 2017). Americans increasingly suspect

DOI: 10.4324/9781003372790-3

mainstream media of bias and are driven to find more objective news sources (Gallup/ Knight Foundation, 2018). Academics, traditional news outlets, and bureaucratic news sources alike are faced with an erosion of trust from the public. Doubts about the accuracy of information are rendered yet more pressing due to the increasing worry that internet platforms act as radicalization pathways. Recommendation algorithms on platforms such as YouTube steer users toward edgier content and clickbait articles remain widely popular in platform-based attention economies. Furthermore, ambivalence and irony pervade online discourse. These cultural structures make it notoriously difficult, if not impossible, to determine authorial intention online. In the present chapter, we trace this particular mode of hermeneutics from the "masters of suspicion," Marx, Freud, and Nietzsche, to the symptomatic readings of Jameson and Althusser, to poststructuralist thought. After outlining the history of this way of thinking and how it manifests itself today, we offer an exemplary, digital-hermeneutic reading of distrust in toxic depression memes.

Suspicion in the History of Hermeneutics

In Chapter 1, we briefly talked about Ricoeur and his distinction of two hermeneutic "modes." But here, we take a step back and ask: how did he come to his ideas on interpretation as a search for double meanings? Ricoeur believed that symbolism and symbolic logic formed the core of all hermeneutics. For him, a symbol is broadly defined as "any structure of signification in which a direct, primary, literal meaning designates, in addition, another meaning which is indirect, secondary and figurative and which can be apprehended only through the first" (2007, 12). Interpretation, then, is deciphering this hidden meaning through thought. Symbols cannot directly be understood because they contain an excess of meaning. Symbol and interpretation logically go together: the multiplicity of meaning necessitates interpretation but is also constituted *in* interpretation.

Such a double meaning can either have the form of an opening to sacred meaning or a dissimulation of meaning, corresponding to the two modes of hermeneutics. The first, which Ricoeur calls hermeneutics of faith, are explored in the next chapter. The second, the hermeneutics of suspicion, is the topic of the present chapter. The first understands interpretation as "manifestation and restoration of meaning"; the latter as "demystification, as a reduction of illusion" (1970, 27). Although Ricoeur is mostly known for combining hermeneutics with phenomenology, which would align him with the former style, he does not take a stand for or against either mode: for him, both strands are equally important and build on each other, as will become clear.

The hermeneutics of suspicion refers to the deconstruction of authority. Where Descartes famously postulated that doubt is pivotal for understanding, thinkers like Marx, Freud, and Nietzsche took a step further and doubted consciousness itself. They understood consciousness as false consciousness since it resides "somewhere else": in the Will to Power for Nietzsche, ideology for Marx, the unconscious, and the libido for Freud. As a result, meaning has been cunningly distorted and it is the task of the critics to reduce the illusions and deceptions of consciousness. Interpretation is then a means to triumph over this doubt by deciphering the expressions of meaning. According to Ricoeur, there is something to be gained from the suspicions of distrust. Freed from false consciousness, we can arrive at a more accurate and humble self-understanding as knowers with limitations. Once our own delusions have been unveiled, we enter the mode of reflection where our interrogations give rise to a quest for understanding, which is where the hermeneutics of faith starts. Structuralism, which came to prominence in the 1960s and '70s, and which drew on developments in linguistics, is also often aligned with this category of suspicious theories, in its postulations of structures lying under the surface of texts.

Eve Kosofsky Sedgwick (2003) uses the term "paranoid reading" for such a critical method characterized by suspicion, vigilance, and a focus on uncovering hidden power structures, meanings, and ideologies. It involves analyzing texts through the lens of suspicion and uncovering repressed or concealed motives. For Sedgwick, paranoia is an epistemological practice— a way of seeking, finding, and organizing knowledge. The paranoid viewer is not surprised to be deceived. Deception is expected, but the surprise and the creativity lie in the specific manner in which it is achieved. Rita Felski (2015) imagines such suspicious readings as acts of "digging down" to reach a hidden reality and thinks of the suspicious critic as an archaeologist who works hard to uncover this valued reality. She argues that the process of false consciousness and the method of deciphering go together: "[t]he man of suspicion carries out in reverse the work of the man of guile" (53). Suspicious readings seek to identify cause-and-effect relations to explain why things happen and assign guilt and blame: they are about *accountability*.

Such practices are a form of symptomatic reading, introduced in our first chapter as the mode of interpretation that takes meaning to be hidden, repressed, deep, and in need of detection and disclosure by an interpreter (Best & Marcus, 2009). The symptomatic reader is vigilant to what is absent in addition to what is present, "reading" with an eye to gaps and ambiguities and viewing "against the grain." After Marx, Freud, and Nietzsche, the most famous examples are Louis Althusser and Étienne Balibar's *Reading Capital* (1965) and Fredric Jameson's *The Political Unconscious* (1981), which were both very influential in the early 1980s. Such works hammered home that we, as subjects, are interpellated by state apparatuses and that everything we do is always already deeply entangled in ideology. "If everything were transparent, then no ideology would be possible, and no domination either," Jameson wrote. This means we can never simply assume that "the text means just what it says." (61). It has been noted that this aggressive, excavating mode of interpretation awards a lot of power to the critic, who is put on a pedestal and is likened to the "God of biblical hermeneutics" with access to truths that mere mortals cannot see (Best & Marcus, 2009, 15).

Practices of paranoid and suspicious hermeneutics originally emerged mostly in English, Philosophy, and other Humanities departments. For Sedgwick, by the early 2000s, "protocols of unveiling [had] become the common currency of cultural and historical studies" (2003, 143). In 2015, Felski still claimed that the ordinary reader's response is marked by a tendency to "take things at face value" (83), which the "heroic" critic would then try to adjust and estrange. Here, our views part. In present-day online culture, the tendency to *not* take things at face value has, on the contrary, become widespread. As we will see, suspicion entails a substantial investment in terms of time, attention, mental energy, and hermeneutic activity, with the assumption that the pay-off is equally substantial.

Fake News and Post-truth (Or: Are We Still Paranoid If They're Really After Us?)

A quick look at the present-day online media landscape might make us wonder if today, suspicion as a default setting is not totally justified. After all, it is hard to deny that deception runs rampant on the internet. Of course, people have always tended to deceive each other for their own gain, but the scale of the Internet and the ability to put any user across the globe into contact with another through instant and anonymous modes of communication have drastically altered our horizons. Fake news is the epistemological crisis of the twenty-first century by excellence. It has upended our notion of the digital public sphere and has collateral effects on our ability to trust what we see and read online. Disinformation and misinformation, extreme speech, clickbait, and propaganda are now all part of the treacherous online ecosystem, which we are still learning to navigate. Increased interaction with algorithms and (autonomous) machines also increase our chances of being manipulated... Alongside human actors with malicious intent or accidental actions are bots that increase the reach of content, spam accounts and click farms that tamper with engagement, and of course algorithms that are designed to calculate how best to manipulate a user's opinions, desires, thoughts, and feelings based on the data they create by interacting with the world online.Another word for this is computational propaganda, or"the assemblage of social media, autonomous agents and algorithms tasked with the manipulation of opinion" (Neudert, 2017, 3). In this context, distrust, or the questioning of the authenticity of other actors, grows into suspicion and then full-blown paranoia.

Fake news was branded as a crisis when it first got its name during the run up to the 2016 US presidential elections. Along with this name came the moral panic; could we ever trust anything again? At the time, it was reported by Buzzfeed news that fake news had outperformed mainstream news on Facebook (Silverman et al., 2016). Amidst a campaign rife with erroneous claims and "alternative facts," fake news emerged as a uniquely digital problem. Online, fake news spread like wildfire, highlighting the very real problems that underlie transposing our opinion-forming processes to a very loosely regulated public sphere. Social networking sites had previously been seen as social networks rather than news distribution platforms. The fake news "crisis," however, changed everything. The financial motivations of platforms in engaging user behavior had not until that moment been thought of as a moral issue. What platforms had been doing for years, engaging users by promoting content, clashed with what many perceived as their civic responsibility in the digital public sphere. Platforms were made to demonstrate a discourse of truth and became the arbiters of veracity. But the rise of the platformized internet also encompasses fringe platforms like Reddit, 4chan, Tumblr, or Discord. The shifting sands of irony and trolling culture that define the grammars of these platforms have made it resistant to interpretation and, thus, put up barriers around the communities that have formed on these platforms, known also as the *ambivalent web* (Phillips & Milner, 2017) or the *vernacular web* (Tuters, 2019).

The vernacular web can be found in the "subcultural depths of the internet," on platforms such as 4chan, 8chan, or Reddit, and is a largely anonymous and pseudonymous culture (Tuters, 2019).[1] Such cultures pride themselves on their abilities to deceive and use the logic of dissimulation to rebel against the so-called identity or authenticity-based platforms such as Facebook and Instagram. Their vernacular is an irony-laden dialect and the irreverent cultural codes that accompany it are meant to satirize a culture they do not see themselves fitting into. On these platforms, vernacular functions both as a collective identification and a protection from outsider scrutiny. The deep vernacular web's intimate and collective dynamics have given rise to substantial misinformation, creating fake news such as the infamous "Pizzagate" conspiracy theory, which made headlines because of its real-life consequences. On 4chan, the idea that a child trafficking ring run by members of the Democratic party was being operated out of a pizza parlor in Washington D.C. had begun to spread. A month later, a man burst into the pizza restaurant with an AR-15 assault rifle, claiming that he wanted to free the child sex slaves he believed the restaurant was harboring. He fired three shots before he was arrested, and later explained his erratic behavior by saying he was self-investigating the conspiracy. This shows that disinformation is not intentional but assembled by a group of actors and the networks on which they collectivize their suspicious hermeneutics. The culture of doubt they generate speaks to what Rosenblum and Muirhead (2019) have coined a "new conspiracism," a shift in conspiratorial thought, where conspiracies are no longer held together by a meaning-making structure but by a general ethic of paranoia. Accusations become the refrain of groups defined by new conspiracism. In these groups, external interference and hyperpartisan actors can mingle with believers to propel along their beliefs. In effect, new conspiracism weaponizes doubt and paranoia and erodes knowledge-making processes and institutions.[2]

Debunking approaches are vital to counter misinformation, while prebunking, for instance, inoculation,[3] can help us detect and classify it. However, an overemphasis on persuasion may reinforce public contestation of expertise. Reasons for mistrusting scientific or academic expertise often go further than a mere misunderstanding or lack of knowledge: emotions and values also play an important role. Sociological studies have shown that even in cases where debunking reveals the falseness of information, people might persist to endorse it for identity-related reasons: "it is not so much the truthfulness of information that counts, but people's social distance to the producers and adjudicators of knowledge" (Harambam, 2021). Invoking human judgment can also lead to error and biases penetrating the seemingly "objective" process of fact-checking. Scholarship on the effectiveness of fact-checking has developed in at least two directions: the extent to which fact-checking corrects the record as well as factual beliefs and whether it changes attitudes (Barrera et al., 2017).

The post-truth condition emerged from this tension between what was deemed "fake" and what was "validated" as true. Post-truth can also be qualified as a disposition toward encountering media or statements *without trust*. In this sense, the post-truth condition is not a debate about first-order objectivity, or the idea of truth existing independent from the individual's judgment, but about second-order objectivity, which is about situating disagreements between a set of actors. Instead of debating what is true, it looks at how different proponents of a debate put forward and legitimate their own objectivity (Venturini, 2012). Harsin (2018), therefore, defines post-truth politics as rationalizing beliefs through one's emotions rather than fact. Affective discourse and engagement played a major part in how propaganda was spread during the election cycle, for instance through memes and irony.

"It was just a meme": Suspicious Readings and Toxic Meme Culture

Many of our online expressions are anonymous, and therefore disembodied: we must get by without the extra information derived from body language, tone, or facial expressions. This makes it hard to determine intentions, as per Poe's Law, the internet adage that holds that "without a clear indication of the author's intent, it is difficult or impossible to tell the difference between an expression of sincere extremism and a parody of extremism" (Phillips & Milner, 2017, 5). Anonymity and pseudonymity are platform affordances that facilitate trolling and satirical, ambivalent play (Phillips & Milner, 2017). This play is not always innocent: in the case of racist or sexist expressions, it is impossible to say if the communicator holds the view in earnest and one can always hide behind "it was just a joke." In *Kill All Normies*, Angela Nagle writes that since 2016, "a spirit of deep nihilistic cynicism and reactive irony bubbled up to the surface of mainstream Internet-culture and an absurd in-jokey forum humor became dominant" (Nagle, 2017, 5).

This is especially the case with memes, which have been cast as both the vessels of participatory networks and the perfect mobilizers of attention. That memes can be powerful weapons became clear in 2016, when they played a prominent role in the online culture wars.[4] Memes are pieces of digital content that circulate online and have become a staple of our online communication. They come in the form of images, texts, videos or, at the root of their definition, simply ideas. We consume them eagerly on platforms like Instagram and integrate them seamlessly into our online conversations. They are designed for humor but have extended their reach way past entertainment and have become a mainstay of political communication and civic life.

Memes are not defined by what they are or how they look, but by how they spread. These units of digital accumulate cultural capital as they circulate, but they are also scalar: a niche subgroup or small community can have memes that are massively influential within their own sphere but inscrutable outside of their meaning making system. Adversely, some memes can take over the world. Memes get their meaning from the cultural practices that circulate around them. They can be recognized and understood even when only a part of their form is recreated. Meaning can be created and changed by replacing the caption or editing the source of the image, for comedic effect for instance. The image is assigned a new signifier every time it is remixed or reappropriated by someone else. Memes are about playing with expectations, including the signifiers that we expect to be tied to certain signifieds through tradition. However, they draw on a semiotic landscape that we are all familiar with so that we can understand them, otherwise they would not go far. This semiotic landscape forms our horizon of interpretation. By keeping the initial format, the meme is still recognizable, yet a new way of interpreting the image or text is born out of editing and remixing. Of course, the longer this process goes on, the harder it is to trace the original. This way, memes become vessels for mediating between the familiar and the strange.

Emblematic of the culture they have come from, memes are polysemous images, meaning they can be interpreted in many ways according to the context that they are encountered in. A meme is part of meme culture, whose aesthetic disposition, tendency to embrace images as comic due to their style, feeds into recent post-truth attitudes online in that it radically accepts irony as a mode of politics. One of the earliest meme scholars, Ryan Milner, presciently wrote that the meme's embrace of irony represented a "hacked social dynamic" as "the blur between irony and earnestness makes room for discourse otherwise impermissible" (2013, 34). This means that linguistic and visual elements of the meme alone do not determine its meaning or how we can interpret it. As the interpretation of memes is infinitely changeable, Gadamer's insights about the horizon of interpretation are particularly relevant for understanding them. The background against which we interpret the meme has cultural significance. We will see how this dialogic process of interpretation helps to uncover parts of the meme that are hidden, not seen at first glance.

Suspicious hermeneuts, however, do not bother entering into a conversation with the text and let this process reach its natural dialogic form, but focus instead on the function of the text as part of this cultural background. In the example we analyze below, we will see how this does a disservice to both the interpreter, the text, and the culture. Introducing new and extreme voices in popular discourse through the memetic medium—harder to moderate because of its shroud of irony—has become another facet of post-truth politics.

Interpreting Images

Images are convincing: they have an affective potential that often overpowers logical or critical thought. Unlike text, people lack an education in critically engaging with images, and "images don't really have counter-arguments" (Finster, 2018). The idea that memes can have an unconscious hold over our patterns of thoughts and opinions is important to take into account in a hermeneutic approach. A meme can go viral and be propagated and spread around without notice being paid to the symbols it contains and the discourses it embodies, creating a mode of thinking that we all mimic. What does this do to our ability to interpret?

Whether an image is to be read ironically or taken at face value depends entirely on its audience and context. The tone of the image is contingent on the habits and cultural practices of the community. A meme coming from a particular subculture will therefore be legible for the people in that group because it will make references to symbolism and imagery that they are familiar with. Consequently, when images are encountered outside of their original community and environment, new meanings are attributed to them and cultural objects can become loaded with symbols that we are unable to trace but that may have particular meanings to some communities. These could be racist or nationalist propaganda spread with harmful intent.[5] Yet, they could also be symbols that are meaningful to marginalized groups and that, when culturally appropriated and depoliticized, provoke harm to this community.

When we study memes hermeneutically, we therefore have to devise an approach that is mindful of, and able to address a number of tensions, including:

i the structural relation between the whole (platform) and its parts (affordances, interface, users, memes),
ii the cultural practices that legitimize texts and delegitimize them as quickly, and
iii the level of literacy or pre-acquired knowledge necessary to understand the memes.

All these digital literacy skills are essential to pull back the layers of a deeply ironic meme. Familiarity with irony is usually acquired after long-term exposure to such a culture, but apart from that, there are some broad principles you can keep in mind which might help uncover and interpret irony. These have to do with an examination of the environment and context. Digital affordances allow us to contextualize text within a platform and a subculture with unique dynamics of production and consumption. On a platform like Tumblr, we can find affordances such as being able to click on the original author of a post, which brings us to a user's post history, where we can perform a close reading in order to assess their tone. We turn our attention now to a case study on Tumblr that shows how interpretations of memes are bound in the context of intimacy, irony, and platform-dependent cultural practices.

Toxic Depression Memes

Depression memes are internet memes that address topics surrounding depressive feelings, anxiety, and low self-esteem and self-worth. Originally subcultural, they breached the mainstream in the late 2010s and have since taken over the internet. The internet's deep familiarity with depressive content has earlier been qualified by one of the authors of this book as a "depression culture" built on the back of an irony-laden approach to mental health (Chateau, 2020). Depression memes were initially lauded as a taboo-breaking way of teaching millennials to address mental health-related issues, "ending stigma by all memes necessary" (Rottenberg, 2014). However, if we believe that digital natives have been conditioned to express and communicate through memes and we take these texts seriously, for instance as lived expertise, a bleak and cynical picture of the next generation emerges. Luckily, they are not to be taken at face value. Playfulness, subversion, and irony affect how seriously we can read a depression meme.

The meme in Figure 2.1 was posted by a user whose account is now deleted and it quickly gained notoriety, amassing almost thirty thousand notes (likes and reblogs) at the time of its circulation. It uses a meme format that originated in 2015 based on a poorly photoshopped image. Here, the joke concerns the user's poor photoshopping skills and comedic public framing of a private situation. It reads "Friendship ended with [Therapy] Now [Venting Online] is my best friend". It showcases remixing and savvy meme knowledge. The post provoked controversy around delicate issues of mental health, therapy, and toxicity. We can see this because the poster felt the need to edit their own post and add a comment:

> *Edit: this is gaining a lot of notes again and i just want to clarify that I'm not anti-therapy or "anti-recovery" or anything*
>
> *This post was me venting about having bad experiences with my last therapist (…)*
>
> *I'm not against therapy …. This post was about a specific bad experience of mine.*

Figure 2.1 A "toxic meme" on tumblr.com.

The exchange indicates that certain criticisms related to "anti-therapy" content had been leveled at the original poster of the meme, either in the notes of the post (comments and reblogs where other users can add text to a post) or in the chat functionality of the website. The author has obviously been held accountable for seemingly propagating what other users saw as "anti-recovery" behavior. What happened, then, is that other users on the platform had an unforeseen interpretation of this meme. Though the poster's aim was to "vent … about a specific bad experience of mine," the meme was approached not just as an object but as a cultural text with a role to play in cultural discourse. Other users picked up on signs in the memes that they believed were part of an "anti-therapy" or "anti-recovery" narrative. This figured in the interpreter's horizon as a narrative that should be looked out for, and, when found, combatted. Being against therapy represented for these users a harmful idea in society that should not be spread—even ironically through a meme. Distrust of the poster's intentions was at the root of this interpretation, which qualifies as a paranoid reading. Such a paranoid approach roots out signs of inauthenticity, especially when couched behind irony, in order to identify what it sees as an inauthentic narrative and replace it with its own, alternative interpretation. True to Gadamer's notion of "foreconception of completeness," the meme is essentially understandable, even if the viewer does not necessarily agree with it. But the interpreters here are not performing "interpretive charity" (Sperber, 2010, 585), or a benevolent reading with the grain, like they would likely do with a communicator that they trusted.

Instead of seeing the meme as a text, they saw it as a symbol or symptom of a toxic cultural discourse. Once it was understood as part of such a "toxic" discourse, its meaning had been fixed. From then on, inscribed in a "problematic" category, no further interpretation was needed and no more efforts at understanding or entering into a relationship with the text were made. Fundamentally, the meme and its response outline the three modes that are presently coexisting on Tumblr and other platforms: (i) a deeply ironic relationship to memes, and simultaneously (ii) not only a self-aware nod to mental illness existing as a culture online but also (iii) accountability and call out culture. If we apply our approach to digital hermeneutics, we arrive at the following analysis.

Platform Hermeneutics

As designed environments that distribute control, platforms are often copyrighted and monetized. These technological environments negotiate forms and levels of privacy and visibility. They offer crucial information that would run the risk of getting "lost in datafication" when on further levels of analysis and interpretation, we extract data from the platform. Platform hermeneutics pays attention to the architecture of the website and what modes of self-expression and social interaction are afforded by it (Van de Ven & Van Nuenen, 2022). When we look at the level of the *interface*, Tumblr is a micro-blogging platform that has a variety of posting functionalities such as photos, text, quotes, videos, audio, as well as chats, and outlinks. This encourages a range of creative formats accessible to all. Users follow any number of blogs, and their content then appears in their dashboard. Tumblr is also an open-source platform that allows for editing and customizing one's blog. This gives users a sense of autonomy and self-determination when it comes to using the platform.

When we look at Tumblr's *affordance*s, the reblogging functionality is perhaps its most discerning and influential one. Reblogging increases the exposure of a post and creates a certain grammar of repetition and virality unique to the platform. Posts are often encountered multiple times, reiterating logics and codes that could be seen as cementing a platform identity. Users are therefore more likely to reproduce grammar and stylistic preferences from other users on the platform, creating a heavily coded subcultural grammar. We can understandgenre conventions born on Tumblr as emanating from affordances such as reblogging that standardize content. Reblogging enhances shared experiences to the extent that Elena Gonzalez-Polledo contends that pain experiences no longer belong to one person on Tumblr. Instead, "by virtue of traveling around the site through reblogging," personal pain experiences are transformed into "symptomatic communication" that "no longer aims to represent or show reality" bound to individual bodies (2016, 7). This way, Yukari Seko and Stephen P. Lewis argue, "such a relatively 'asocial' affordance of Tumblr has made it particularly conducive to performing non-normative subjectivities" (2018, 182).

When we consider the platform's *governmentality*, Tumblr users' approach toward the platform owners is historically contingent on the site's reputation as subpar and dysfunctional social media site. Compared to the successes of Facebook, Instagram or X, Tumblr's place has always been on the fringes of internet culture. As a website, its structure and interface make it so that accurate advertising and targeted content are almost unachievable. As a result, Tumblr is not a marketable platform. In fact, the site lost 99.8% of its value from 2013 to now. Related to this, the site is often referred to as "broken," with its functionalities being extremely restrictive and infrequently updated. Many users use plug-ins (additional applications that enhance the experience with more functionalities) to use the site. For example, its sorting algorithm has never changed from a chronological ordering to a more interest-based one, as Facebook, X, and Instagram have all done. In this way, it is perceived as the last bastion of a pre-marketable platform. Because of this, Tumblr users often feel more protective of the space and perceive it as a remaining subcultural beacon in the larger platformized web.

In terms of *identity* or *pseudo-/anonymity*, Tumblr users choose a pseudonym for their blog that becomes the username they use when interacting on the platform. However, it is also conventional for users to have their real names in the personal biography section of their blog, and for other users to refer to them using their name. Additionally, an anonymous function is available when sending "asks" to other blogs. This anonymity leaves the door open for a strong call-out culture on Tumblr, as we see in our example.

Cultural Practices

Though Tumblr is not an identity-based platform, *authenticity* is still a relevant concept to understand user interaction. Tumblr's strong platform identity, and affordances, presents a fecund space for the reception and curation of "othered" identities. Due to this, political awareness becomes one of the pillars of identity formation on Tumblr. A strong sense of kinship has cultivated a learning and teaching culture for Tumblr users, where educational and informational content is spread through reblogging and a sense of social cohesion is manipulated to keep users accountable when in the wrong. Accountability is a recurring concern, but this comes from a place of normative intimacy, where users are expected to follow certain codes and norms in order to respect and safeguard each other's identities and values. Subversion is another aspect that sets apart the platform: Tumblr's reputation is that of a liberal online culture "successful in pushing fringe ideas into the mainstream" (Nagel, 2017, 68). The platform has incited not only academic attention in its formulation and performance of feminism but also queer aesthetics and queer social justice. As a space, it disrupts hegemonic ideas.

Literacy

Tumblr has primarily be known as a place for humor, where many memes have seen the light of day. However, many of these have tended to stay on the platform rather than leak out. When considering platforms like Twitter/X, Instagram or Facebook, content is often reposted from one to the other. Much content then overlaps, giving these platforms a sense of sharing the same identity or approach to humor or content. Though Tumblr content is often reposted on other platforms, like Reddit, this reposting is often treated as a form of commentary. Rather than being seamlessly integrated into the platform it is reposted onto, a differentiation is made between Tumblr and Reddit culture. This can be seen in the subreddit r/TumblrInAction, which has a mass following dedicated to identifying throughout the internet, not just on Tumblr, evidence of points of view misrepresenting or overemphasizing political correctness to an extreme degree. In this grammar, "TumblrInAction" refers to identity politics becoming a satire of itself. Therefore, the platform culture and humor profile (including irony) of Tumblr is more singular than some other platforms. The codeification of humor can be traced back to its unique affordances and practices.

It is notable that Tumblr content stays in circulation on the platform for years due to its reblogging economy. However, no dates are given on a post when encountered in a user's feed, only when they are traced back to the original blog. Therefore, a strong sense of anachronism messes with how to interpret ironic content or memes. It is more difficult to tell if an ironic meme has been posted when still edgy, or after a certain meme trend has peaked and irony is now the dominant form of approaching it. The different discourses in circulation on the platform can thus often clash.

Finally, what subcultures and discourses is a meme like this tapping into when published on a platform like Tumblr? Given everything outlined above, we can draw out accountability, social justice, and political awareness as discourses relevant to analyzing this meme. Clearly, humor, personal expression, and catharsis were the intention here. Unfortunately, the medium of the meme contains within its structural grammar components of relatability and spreadability, which signify that personal expression can often be at odds with choosing this medium. At the same time, the author was held accountable for contributing to a negative dialogue around mental health and accused of being "anti-recovery," when theirs was simply one of many contributions to a popular form of discourse on the platform. Similar memes exist, and are widespread, but here, due to the structures of normative intimacy in place on the platform, corresponding more with pedagogy, safeguarding, and wokeness, the author was held accountable. Though humor, personal expression, and catharsis were the intention, irony taken authentically breached the norms of the discursive repertoires on the platform and became "toxic." This is an example of a paranoid reading that stems from the particular platform culture and affordances of Tumblr and operationalizes a hermeneutic of suspicion to read this meme "against the grain."

Conclusion

As Hugo Mercier writes in *Not Born Yesterday: The Science of Who we Trust and What we Believe*, we are far from gullible. Judged by contemporary online practices, we could perhaps even stand to be a little more trusting. However, this is not an easy feat when deception and ambiguity run rampant. Paraphrasing Joseph Heller's *Catch-22*, the old question arose: is it still paranoia when they are really out to deceive you? Or can we see a present-day suspicious hermeneutic as an almost natural response? Indeed, a hermeneutics of suspicion deeply informs online spheres in the form of conspiracy discourses, the encoding of languages of marginalization and systemic oppression in political discourse (e.g., dog whistles), and a prevalent logic of accountability on social media. We see this clearly in the pervasiveness of metaphors of alienation, sleep and awakening, from the "far left" to the "far right"—from "woke" ideologies to the "red pill" and the automated ways of living of the "sheep" who blindly followed their national pandemic protocols. Each group understands the self as awake among the sleeping and the ignorant, attuned to what is "really going on." Paranoia and deception are now so closely interrelated that they become hard to disentangle.

On a positive note, this also means that practices of close reading and close viewing are alive and kicking. We address such practices at more length in our next chapter on the hermeneutics of faith, but this can be considered a somewhat arbitrary choice since, as we have seen, close reading is a form of scrutiny that is just as much associated with distrust as with trust. Whereas such skills are an indispensable and invaluable part of citizen's media literacy, they can have dire consequences when used for "paranoid" ends and when truth-seeking becomes a personal responsibility within a culture of doubt and critique.

Media literacy became one of the solutions that Humanities scholars promoted as an antidote to the post-truth condition, understood as a way to empower users to take a more active role in interpreting online content. The ability to critically analyze structure, tone, author, representation, and other factors would increase citizen's resilience, counter extremism, and deweaponize propaganda. Media literacy education centers on teaching students how to critically question sources and senders' motivation, but we now see how it has been influenced by the tenets of post-truth politics, and proposed as its antidote. boyd argues (2017) that a well-intended emphasis on fact checking on the part of journalistic media and educators as a solution to misinformation might have the inadvertent effect of suggesting that in complex global, socio-political issues, there is always a singular truth, or one legitimate worldview out there, waiting to be found (boyd, 2017; 2018). She argues that media literacy, when understood as individual truth-finding, promotes self-segregating, experience over expertise and a culture of doubt, which are the precise conditions that have led to the post-truth climate in the first place.

In order to address this, our hermeneutic approach has stressed the importance of context. We have seen that interpretation should not stop at the level of the utterance, the text or image, but should take platform culture and affordances into account. Because of their scalar quality, we have seen, memes can obtain meaning and capital in very specific contexts, which does not necessarily translate to other contexts, underlining the importance of horizons of interpretation. The proliferation of online spheres has not led to a huge fusion of horizons, but rather to a seemingly infinite fragmentation, along other than the "traditional," geographic, or historical, lines. Memes are excellent vessels for playing with expectations and mediating between familiar and strange, but they have also become an intrinsic part of post-truth politics because of their polysemous nature, their notoriously slippery meaning. The cultural narratives that dominate a platform or subculture may completely clash with mainstream discourses: indeed, that may be the reason they exist. In many ways, this can entail a valuable production of counter-knowledge with the potential to disrupt hegemony in productive ways. However, it can also backfire. Many of us are media literate, but what if this literacy is used in the service of paranoia and leads to extremism or call-out culture?

As Ricoeur stressed, interpretation—understood as deciphering hidden meanings—becomes necessary because meanings are always already multiple. Irony and trolling, as staples of the ambivalent or vernacular web, both necessitate and resist interpretation. Our layered interpretation of a toxic depression meme has teased out these dynamics in practice. In our example, we have seen how they can lead to paranoid communities of interpretation in which suspicious readings dig for causal relations, project negative intent, and try to then assign blame and demand accountability. Rather than engaging in a productive conversation with the text, such a reading sees the text as a *symptom* for culture. We will now see that something rather different is at stake when we consider the other mode of interpretation distinguished by Ricoeur: the hermeneutics of faith.

Notes

1 Tuters' use of this concept should be differentiated from that by net-art pioneer Olia Lialina, who has been using the phrase "vernacular web" for years in her work that mines the riches of her archive of Geocities sites from the early days of the Web (see for instance "Vernacular Web 2," http://contemporary-home-computing.org/vernacular-web-2/).
2 The effect of conspiratorial thinking, once it ceases to function as any sort of explanation, is delegitimation. The new conspiracist accusations seek not only to unmask and disempower those they accuse but to deny their standing to argue, explain,

persuade, and decide. Conspiracism rejects their authority. In the end, the consequences of delegitimation are not targeted or discrete but encompassing.

3 Based on an analogy with immunology, inoculation theory holds that preventively
exposing people to a weakened version of deceptive information would prompt a
thought process that is equivalent to developing "mental antibodies," rendering the
recipients immune to misleading attempts at persuasion (Van der Linden & Roozenbeek, 2020).

4 The online culture wars took place in the early 2010s and are said to have resulted
in the rise of the alt-right which played a major role in the presidential election of
Donald Trump (Nagle, 2017). See for a visual map of these culture wars, consist-
ing of an overlay of hundreds of politicized memes, including influential political
figures and symbols: https://disnovation.org/ocw.php.

5 Many racist symbols were hidden in the memes and images circulating around
the 2016 US President elections, i.e. the number 88 is a white supremacist symbol
standing for "Heil Hitler," as well as the number 14, both are often combined in
various forms. Imagery such as racist caricatures have also been known to form
the basis of memes, which, when decontextualized, are not interpreted as racist
anymore but simply a meme format.

References

Althusser, L., & Balibar, E. (1970). *Reading Capital* (B. Brewster Trans). New York
(NY): New Left Books.

Barrera, O., Guriev, S., Henry, E., & Zhuravskaya, E. (2020). Facts, Alternative Facts,
and Fact Checking in Times of Post-Truth Politics. *Journal of Public Economics*,
182 (2020), 104–123.

Bialik, K., & Matsa, K. E. (2017). Key Trends in Social and Digital News Media. *Pew
Research Center*, 4–10.

boyd, d. (2017). Did Media Literacy Backfire? *Journal of Applied Youth Studies*, 1(4),
83–89.

boyd, d. (2018, March 9). You Think You Want Media Literacy… Do You? *Zephoria*. https://www.zephoria.org/thoughts/archives/2018/03/09/you-think-you-want-
media-literacy-do-you.html

Chateau, L. (2020). 'Damn I Didn't Know Y'all Was Sad? I Thought It Was Just
Memes' Irony, Memes and Risk in Internet Depression Culture. *M/C Journal*, 23(3).
DOI: 10.5204/mcj.1654

Felski, R. (2015). *The Limits of Critique*. Chicago (IL): The University of Chicago
Press.

Finster, T. (2018, August 6). Everybody Thinks in Memes Now. *Dazed*. http://www.
dazeddigital.com/life-culture/article/40583/1/memethink-genexit-box1824-
report-normcore-memes

Gallup/Knight Foundation. (2018). American Views: Trust, Media and Democracy.
Knight Foundation Report. https://knightfoundation.org/wp-content/uploads/2022/10/
American-Views-2022-pt1.pdf

Gonzalez-Polledo, E. (2016). Chronic Media Worlds: Social Media and the Problem of Pain Communication on Tumblr. *Social Media + Society*, 1–11. DOI:
10.1177/2056305116628887

Harambam, J. (2021). Against Modernist Illusions: Why We Need More Democratic
and Constructivist Alternatives to Debunking Conspiracy Theories. *Journal for Cultural Research*, 25(1), 104–122. DOI: 10.1080/14797585.2021.1886424

Harsin, J. (2018). Post-Truth and Critical Communication Studies. *Oxford Research Encyclopedia of Communication*. DOI: 10.1093/acrefore/9780190228613.013.757

Jameson, F. (1981). *The Political Unconscious: Narrative as a Socially Symbolic Act*. Ithaca, NY: Cornell University Press.

Lialina, O. Vernacular Web 2. http://www.contemporary-home-computing.org/vernacular-web-2/

van der Linden, S., & Roozenbeek, J. (2020). Psychological Inoculation against Fake News. In Greifeneder, R., Jaffé, M. E., Newman, E. J., and Schwarz, N. (Eds.), *The Psychology of Fake News: Accepting, Sharing, and Correcting Misinformation*, (pp. 147–169). New York and London: Routledge.

Mercier, H. (2020). *Not Born Yesterday. The Science of Who We Trust and What We Believe*. Princeton and Oxford: Princeton University Press.

Milner, R. M. (2013). Pop Polyvocality: Internet Memes, Public Participation, and the Occupy Wall Street Movement. *International Journal of Communication*, 7, 2357–2390.

Nagle, A. (2017). *Kill All Normies. Online Culture Wars from 4chan and Tumblr to Trump and the Alt-Right*. Winchester, UK: Zero Books.

Neudert, L. N. (2017). Computational Propaganda in Germany: A Cautionary Tale. *Computational Propaganda Research Project*, Working Paper 7.

Phillips, W., & Milner, R. M. (2017). *The Ambivalent Internet: Mischief, Oddity and Antagonism Online*. Hoboken, NJ: John Wiley & Sons.

Ricoeur, P. (1970). *Freud and Philosophy: An Essay on Interpretation* (D. Savage Trans). New Haven, CT: Yale University Press.

Rosenblum, N. L., & Muirhead, R. (2019). *A Lot of People Are Saying: The New Conspiracism and the Assault on Democracy*. Princeton, NJ: Princeton University Press.

Rottenberg, J. (2014, April 10). Ending Stigma by All Memes Necessary. *Huffington Post*. https://www.huffingtonpost.com/jonathan-rottenberg/depression-stigma_b_5108140.html

Sedgwick, E. K. (2003). *Touching Feeling: Affect, Pedagogy, Performativity*. Durham, NC: Duke University Press.

Seko, Y., & Lewis, S. P. (2018). The Self—Harmed, Visualized, and Reblogged: Remaking of Self-Injury Narratives on Tumblr. *New Media & Society*, 20(1), 180–198.

Silverman, C., et al. (2016). Hyperpartisan Facebook Pages Are Publishing False and Misleading Information at an Alarming Rate. *Buzzfeed News*. https://www.buzzfeed.com/craigsilverman/partisan-fbpages-analysis

Sperber, D. (2010). The Guru Effect. *Review of Philosophical Psychology*, 1(4), 583–592. DOI: 10.1007/s13164-010-0025-0

Tuters, M. (2019). LARPing & Liberal Tears: Irony, Belief and Idiocy in the Deep Vernacular Web. In M. Fielitz, & Thurston, N. (Eds.), *Post-Digital Cultures of the Far Right* (pp. 37–48). Bielefeld: Transcript Verlag.

Van de Ven, I., & Van Nuenen, T. (2022). Digital Hermeneutics: Scaled Readings of Online Depression Discourses. *Medical Humanities*, 48(3), 335–346. DOI: 10.1136/medhum-2020-012104

Venturini, T. (2012). Building on Faults: How to Represent Controversies with Digital Methods. *Public Understanding of Science*, 21(7), 796–812. DOI: 10.1177/0963662510387558

3 Especially For You
Hermeneutics of Faith

Doing the Research Yourself: The Problem with Trust

A popular narrative ascribes the (for many) surprising electoral success of Donald Trump in 2016 at least in part to Facebook's algorithms. The story goes that the platform facilitated the viral spread of a campaign that hinged on fake news, basically brainwashing people into voting for Trump. However, *The Propagandist Playbook* (2022) by media studies scholar Francesca Tripodi tells a different picture. Tripodi attended Republican events associated with two upper-middle-class evangelical communities in the Southeastern United States in 2017 and did fieldwork by shadowing them on- and offline and conducting in-depth interviews. As it turned out, these groups did not trust social media any more than they did mainstream media. Instead of relying on such intermediaries, they went straight to 'the source' itself, consuming Trump's speeches, videos, and Tweets by using the same critical methods of reading and interpreting as they applied when studying the Bible, and then discussing them together. What was this if not media literacy? They were certainly 'doing the research' themselves:

> they consumed a great deal of information and found inconsistencies, not within the words of Trump himself, but rather within the way mainstream media 'twisted his words' to fit a narrative they did not agree with. Not unlike their Protestant ancestors, doing so gave them authority over the text rather than relying on the priests' (i.e., 'the elites'') potentially corrupt interpretation.
>
> (Tripodi, 2018)

Tripodi concluded that these upper-middle class conservatives did not vote for Trump because they were 'deceived' by 'fake news.' The evangelicals are close readers par excellence since they have been taught at church to read the Bible in its original form, rather than to rely on what other people and media authorities say. They distrust intermediaries but thereby put *a lot* of trust in the author himself.

DOI: 10.4324/9781003372790-4

Where our last chapter focused on distrusting or suspicious styles of interpretation, this chapter deals with the opposite situation, which is just as amply represented in online culture, namely interpretations that stem from an overly trusting and uncritical stance toward technology, celebrities, and other users from the same community. Unlike distrust, trust is generally considered a good thing, indeed indispensable for living together in society and for our basic survival, but it can become too much of a good thing when it turns into blind trust. We can, for instance, be too trusting of the platforms that govern our interactions, algorithms that make choices for us, intellectual gurus, influencers, and people who think the same as we do. And more often than not, this is actively afforded by the technologies we use. In this chapter, we explore a range of technological manifestations of this phenomenon, including algorithmic biases, echo chambers, and filter bubbles, which we interrelate with psychological phenomena related to trust like confirmation bias.

But first, we once more turn to the history of this mode of interpretation in hermeneutic tradition. Ricoeur contrasts the hermeneutics of suspicion with readers who come at a text with hopes of revelation. He identifies this strand of hermeneutics in the phenomenology of religion and its symbolic language. As in the hermeneutics of suspicion, meaning is considered disguised and distorted in these linguistic and cultural expressions. However, rather than 'excavating' or subverting it in a hostile manner, the interpreter feels herself addressed by the text and unveils its meaning with an attitude of reverence, according to a logic of revelation. We take New Criticism's close reading and reparative readings (Sedgwick) to belong to this hermeneutics as well. We then trace this hermeneutics of faith, trust, or restoration in the context of contemporary practices in online culture, including online fandom, echo chambers, and filter bubbles. We discuss the vital role that trust plays on the level of platform infrastructure and in relation to algorithms. After outlining these issues, we apply an exemplary digital-hermeneutic reading of the role of trust in online discussions of the already notorious case of the defamation trial of Johnny Depp versus Amber Heard.

'Believing to Understand, Understanding to Believe'

As became clear in Chapter 1, the roots of philosophical hermeneutics can be found in the medieval religious hermeneutics invented to systematize the exegesis of the Holy Bible. This approach revolves around what is called the 'fourfold senses' of the biblical Scriptures: the literal, the allegorical, the moral, and the anagogical. Dante calls this the 'allegory of theologians,' according to which he structured his *Divine Comedy*. The literal, historical meaning of the Old Testament was read spiritually in light of the New Testament. Bible exegesis was already a reflexive exercise in which the reader learned something about herself. Each reader derived a different meaning from the text which could be related to her own situation in the here and now (Fawzy, 2018).

Ricoeur's hermeneutics was deeply influenced by this tradition. Ricoeur focuses on the ontological dimension of language, which, according to him, turns the text into a mirror in which the reader can see herself reflected and understand both self and world. The spiritual meaning of the text is only fully realized when the reader interiorizes it and makes it her own, which Ricoeur called the "mutual interpretation of Scripture and existence" (2007, 384). For him, as for Heidegger and Gadamer, interpretation is not just an epistemological exercise or a mode of knowing but also, or primarily, an ontological one: a mode of being. Rather than a reconstruction of the text's original meaning, it is about self-understanding, or understanding the self *through* the text. Understanding the self and existence should start with language, the "level on which understanding takes place" (Ricoeur, 2007, 10). Because Ricoeur believes that all language is symbolic, symbolism is "the privileged theme of the hermeneutic field" (1970, 8). Ricoeur's theory on text and interpretation deals with an excess of meaning and poses "a question of the plurivocity belonging to full works of discourse, such as poems, narratives, and essays" (1976, xi). The symbol carries a multiplicity of meanings. It is therefore always in need of interpretation, be it from an attitude of suspicion or of faith.

In *Freud and Philosophy*, Ricoeur contrasts the suspicious interpreter to the reader who approaches the text from the hope of experiencing a revelation from it. Again, 'what you see' is not 'what you get.' Meaning is disguised but in a different sense. Rather than trying to subvert the text and expose its underlying hierarchies, the reader revels in the fullness and complexities of language, where the latent meaning inhabits the manifest meaning. The emphasis is on presence rather than what the text hides. Interpretation in this mode is not about authorial intention. It is about believing and trusting that the object contained within the symbol wants to be revealed and can function as a potential gateway to sacred meanings. This attitude is, however, not to be confused with a blind trust or naive faith. It rather entails 'a rational faith' that, by interpreting, traverses the hermeneutic circle, a movement that Ricoeur describes as "[b]elieve in order to understand, understand in order to believe" (1970, 28). For the phenomenology of religion, symbols are the sensible manifestation of a depth or a form of truth that is not directly accessible. They show and hide their double meanings at the same time, revealing the sacred. The text opens itself up to the reader, whose interpretation restores its meaning.

In this process, the reader feels herself addressed by the text as if it was a message sent specifically to her. As its words reveal truth rather than hide it, the interpretative act is an unveiling, not an unmasking. Such a hermeneutics of faith, or restoration, is, in Rita Felski's words, full of "moments of wonder, reverence, exaltation, hope, epiphany, or joy" (2015, 32). Ricoeur identifies it in the phenomenology of religion, in dreams, and the poetic imagination. Where psychoanalysis demystifies discourse, phenomenology remythicizes it. Both modes of interpretation do not cancel each other out. They can, and should, be combined: where the hermeneutics of suspicion deconstructs the symbolic, the hermeneutics of faith entails the restoration and reconstruction of meaning *despite* all possible suspicion.

Restore, Repair, or Let It Be: Reading Surfaces

Just like the hermeneutics of suspicion did not die with Marx, Freud, and Nietzsche, traces of the hermeneutics of faith can be seen back in modern hermeneutics as well, most often as a counter-response to more hostile and aggressive or 'excavating' modes of interpretation. In Chapter 1, we have already addressed some of these approaches, which have in common that they all go against 'symptomatic' modes of reading. Here, we discuss them at more length insofar as they seek to re-establish faith and meaning to the text.

Sontag, as mentioned before, was one of the first to condemn the hermeneutics of suspicion for replacing the work of art with interpretation. In her manifesto "Against Interpretation" (1966), she also reflects on criticism that would mitigate such aggressive acts. Instead of paraphrasing content, she makes a case for attention to form and formalism, in a descriptive rather than prescriptive tone: "acts of criticism which would supply a really accurate, sharp, loving description of the appearance of a work of art" (2001, 9). She urges art critics to prioritize *transparency* over depth, layers, and meaning, showing "the luminousness of the thing itself." In moderate, secularized form, we can still see a little bit of the sacred here that Ricoeur wrote about. This thing itself, Sontag contends, is meant to be experienced through the senses. In place of a hermeneutics, she states, "we need an erotics of art" (14).

Heather Love stated that even if the analysis of texts and culture has been secularized in the course of the twentieth century and we do no longer perceive 'the message' to be divine, literary interpretation has not shaken off the notion of 'the opacity and ineffability of the text and the ethical demand to attend to it' (Love, 2010, 371), which remain quite central to its practices. Some of the more 'sacred' aspects and humanistic values, she feels, still linger in contemporary hermeneutics. This, according to Love, is primarily due to close reading still being a core business of hermeneutics and a central method of literary studies. Love turns to sociology, a discipline which, like literary studies, engages in practices of close attention, but relies on description rather than interpretation, which helps researchers to leave humanistic and metaphysical assumptions at the door. Inspired by Bruno Latour and Erving Goffman, her solution is to "develop modes of reading that are close but not deep" (2010). 'Thin description' can be seen as such a mode or reading method that uses techniques that were originally developed to analyze patterns of behavior and visible activity. She argues that anthropologist Clifford Geertz, who adapted the notion of thick description for the social sciences, thereby applied to ethnography what was in fact a literary studies method. In contrast to thick description, a reading that imbues a text, behavior, or cultural object with layers of meaning, depth, and intention, thin description entails "an unadorned, first-order account of behavior, one that could be recorded just as well by a camera as by a human agent" (2013, 403). Applied to literature, it is a way to avoid speculation about interiority, meaning, or depth.

Eve Kosofsky Sedgwick (2003) proposes reparative reading as a counterpoint to suspicion. Inspired by psychoanalytic theory (especially the work of Melanie Klein) and the affect theory of Silvan Tomkins, reparative reading is foremost an ethical attempt to reassemble or 'repair' the parts of a text or phenomenon that were taken apart by more aggressive modes of interpretation, not necessarily to a pre-existing whole, but to a new whole. Unlike the paranoid stance marked by knowingness, the reparative reader has an open attitude toward the possibility of surprise and even hope. In this new constitution, the interpreter might then identify with the resulting object, and it might even offer comfort in the face of trauma.

Last, Sharon Marcus and Stephen Best coined the term 'surface reading' to describe a collection of approaches that have in common that they attend to the elements of a text that are obvious and 'in your face,' and take these elements at face value. Countering symptomatic reading, such a surface reading tries to take the text literally and moves 'with the grain.' It considers what is present, rather than what texts withhold:

> [W]e take surface to mean what is evident, perceptible, apprehensible in texts; what is neither hidden nor hiding; what, in the geometrical sense, has length and breadth but no thickness, and therefore covers no depth. A surface is what insists on being looked at rather than what we must train ourselves to see through.
>
> (2009, 9)

The underlying (no pun intended) assumption of surface reading is that texts reveal their own truths and do not need critics to do this: what we think that theory does is already present in them.[1] The effect of depth lies in the surface, is simply a continuation of it, and therefore an effect of immanence. Replacing 'heroic' exercises of interpretation, where the interpreter saves the day by doing the important work of disclosing what the text is 'really' about, the surface reader simply describes what is *already there*. Marcus demonstrates this approach, which she also calls this "just reading" (2007, 75), through an interpretation of female friendship in Victorian novels, not as a stand-in for censored lesbian desire but as actual female friendship. Surface reading is (somewhat paradoxically) described as valuing immersion and should be undertaken with an attitude of openness, receptiveness, and attentiveness.

In sum, reparative and restorative practices of reading pay close attention to surfaces and present this as an ethical and affective posture. The attitude toward the text is one of acceptance, not mastery or instrumentalism: a close, attentive reading that nevertheless does not assume or project depth. These approaches have been critiqued for being apolitical and uncritical and thus accepting the status quo. Countering such allegations, Sedgwick stresses that the reparative practices she advocates by no means deny systematic oppression in the world. To refuse the paranoid stance does not necessarily mean to be naive, complacent, or quietist (2003, 150).

We have reviewed these approaches in this section because we believe that even though they try to go against 'depth hermeneutics,' their decision *not* to interpret from a position of suspicion betrays a certain level of trust in the text.[2] A surface reading trusts that the text is honest about what it is trying to communicate, that it has no hidden meanings, or if it has, that they somehow 'shine through' and reveal themselves to the attentive reader. We see a mix of the hermeneutics of faith and an attempt at post-hermeneutics here. But would one surface-read or thinly describe a work of art with less than wholesome content? What about non-fictional online discourse, where intent is difficult to pinpoint? We think that restorative practices imply a valuation and a pre-selection of what is deemed worthy of being restored or repaired. This is where trust comes in. Even though Best and Marcus say they refuse to celebrate or condemn their objects of study (2009, 18), *not* condemning something would not in all cases be desirable or appropriate. All proponents of these reading practices tend to select case studies that they are implicitly positive about, which implies a relation of trust.

Sticking to the Words on the Page: Close Reading

Despite their disavowal of depth hermeneutics, most of these approaches still lend a crucial role to close reading. Ricoeur even writes that hermeneutics itself, the art of reading carefully, is a school of patience (Grondin, 2015, 150). Close reading is an umbrella term for an assortment of reading strategies characterized by a devout and detailed attention to the meaning and composition of artworks. It plays an important role in both the hermeneutics of suspicion and that of faith, but we choose to discuss it at more length in this chapter because of its special relation to trust. The approach was made famous by the New Critics, a group of Anglo-American literary scholars including Cleanth Brooks, William K. Wimsatt, and Monroe C. Beardsley, who experienced their heyday in the forties and fifties of the last century.

In the 1920s, the Cambridge critic I.A. Richards held a series of 'experiments' on which he reported in *Practical Criticism* (1929). He presented his students with a number of poems, without giving them any contextual information, including the author's name and the year of publication. He did this because he wanted to encourage his students to concentrate exclusively on the words on the page ("nothing but the bare words before him on the paper," 4) rather than leaning on ideas they already might have had about the text—what Gadamer would call prejudice. This form of close analysis, Richards believed, would have psychological benefits. It allowed them to come to a sharp analysis of both the currents of thought in the poem and their own emotional responses to it. In *Seven Types of Ambiguity* (1930), Richards' student William Empson studied the complex and multifarious meanings of poems. The work of both these scholars profoundly influenced the New Criticism, whose proponents saw poems as intricate structures of meaning.

Going against contemporary practices that, in their view, overvalued historical context and biographical information, the New Critics criticized certain contemporary 'fallacies' of literary analysis, for instance, letting your own emotions factor into the interpretation (Wimsatt & Beardsley's "affective fallacy," 1949) or writing about authorial intentions (the "intentional fallacy," Wimsatt & Beardsley, 1946). Another practice they denounced was the paraphrasing of the contents or 'message' of a work (Brooks' "Heresy of Paraphrase," 1947). Inspired by Richards, they suggested that literary scholars should investigate *the text itself*—its images, symbols, and metaphors—as part of a larger structure that gives the text its unity and meaning. Form and content cannot really be separated, because the reading experience, including the unresolved tensions in the text, give the poem its meaning. Words and references in a poem or literary texts are often ambiguous and carry multiple meanings that enhance a reader's valuation of the work (Empson, 1930).

Perhaps none too surprisingly, the 1960s saw the downfall of this textual approach (but only in its purest form). Besides being considered elitist (solely focused on complex, 'high-end' texts) and intellectualist (favoring intricate and dense interpretations and treating the text as a puzzle to be solved), the New Criticism was deemed too restrictive. It did not allow for considerations of race, class, gender, emotions, the author, reader response, socio-historical context, and ideology—all categories that moved to the center of literary studies in the sixties. Yet these last decades, it seems ready for a revival. The term is brought up more frequently, mostly in opposition to 'newer' practices like distant reading (Van de Ven, 2018) or hyper-reading (Hayles, 2012; Van de Ven, 2023). Authors like Michael Manderino (2015) and Antoine Compagnon (2014) attempt to rehabilitate close reading and its devotion to detail, arguing that we need these skills more than ever in times of information overload. We believe that close reading was never really left behind and that, more importantly, when we look at online culture today, it seems *everyone* is doing it. What is different from the time of the New Critics, who applied this approach to a small canon of literature, is the context of online culture with its abundance of information on the one hand and a number of measures to counter and filter overload on the other.

Trust in Platforms and Online Communities

So far, we have been discussing the hermeneutics of faith foremost in relation to hermeneutic *strategies*. However, trust in texts and other cultural expressions is not just connected to modes and strategies of reading, but also to environments. In this context, we will now see how online spaces are often designed to connect us to people whom we already trust. Whereas they once held a promise for democratic deliberation, these spaces are now often said to threaten it. It is therefore important to also look at trust in the platforms that enable the emergence of communities of trust. The invention of the internet in the twentieth century was accompanied by an idealistic belief in its connective power called the Californian Ideology: the belief that the horizontal communication that the web enabled would give everyone a voice. Yet, as the weight of the web's presence in our lives increased, critics have warned that instead of offering a space for deliberative democracy between connected citizens, the net would instead likely be shaped by the existing entrenched social and economic power relations of contemporary societies (Hill & Hughes, 1998). This era saw many critiques of platforms, ownership, and the 'digital divide' (Dahlberg, 2001; 2005; Fuchs, 2014). Gradually, critics started to realize that rather than democratization, web 2.0 led to ideological segregation, which is of the main dangers to deliberative communication online and one of the main obstacles to understanding. The forming of personalized information environments that filter out unwanted content leads to selective exposure (Freelon, 2015).

Filter bubbles are ideologically cohesive spaces created by recommendation and personalization algorithms, which analyze users' online activity and interests and then expose them to content that echoes with it, resulting in a lack of exposure to ideologically diverse content (Pariser, 2011). Such filtering may shape echo chambers when socializing with like-minded groups and individuals and the avoidance of counter-attitudinal material reinforce the world views of a particular ideological group. A notorious example is the aforementioned fanbase of Trump. In the case study for this chapter, we will see how Reddit, with its organization in subreddits, invites users to come together around topics within clearly delineated spaces, each with its own rules for content and behavior. Subreddits can promote or even require echo chamber activities when they advance participation among a group of like-minded users while excluding outsiders (Guest, 2018). When there is little opportunity for introducing new or opposing views, the shared views start to reverberate and 'echo' around the chamber, becoming gradually reinforced, which leads to polarization: opposing groups start to lose all common ground. Besides subreddits, examples include community blogs but also X, which enables users to tune in to information streams of their choice through individualized timelines and hashtags (Freelon, 2015; Karpf, 2012). This is problematic since exposure to a diverse range of sources is considered conducive to democracy, while exclusive access to opinion-reinforcing content may lead to 'cyberbalkanization,' the fragmentation of online spaces.

In order to draw attention to the role of trust in these mechanisms and to look at trust not just in regards to members of our own communities but also in the platforms that facilitate building these communities, it is important to address the tension between private and public spheres which structures many of our online interactions. Platforms obviously need to obtain our trust for their business model to work. The question of trust in their algorithms closely relates to a need for interpretability, which becomes a precondition for trust, for instance with the personalization of news on platforms. We put considerable trust in search engine and may blindly trust results from platforms that rely on algorithms without understanding the potential biases that influence the outcome.[3] Informed by privacy concerns, algorithmic news platforms are increasingly called upon to reveal their justifications for how their results are arrived at through algorithmic gatekeeping, what types of data have been used, and how these have been processed and analyzed (Shin et al., 2022). Interpretability is an important aspect of such explanations and legitimizations. It helps users understand the algorithms, which establishes or enhances trust in news platformization. User trust in algorithmic contexts is greatly influenced by values like transparency, accountability, and fairness.

But even regardless of these factors, algorithms have come to be seen as powerful tools for making sense of the world. In fact, in some cases, people trust algorithms more than humans to make decisions for them (Shin et al., 2022). When previously 'subjective' tasks are deemed quantifiable and based on measurable data, this typically increases the media users' trust in algorithms to perform those tasks, which are then seen as reliable due to their perceived objectivity. This includes feeding us knowledge about ourselves: many people have embraced data-driven ways of knowing in their personal lives, for instance through self-tracking as a way to know themselves physically and mentally. Tracking apps and dating apps help us synthesize patterns from numerous data points in ways that would be impossible without algorithms. This makes people trust algorithms to reveal to them things about themselves that they cannot see and to offer them things they need or want, even before they consciously know what they want. When there is a sense that the desired kind of content will find *us*, the interpretive agency is outsourced to algorithms. Often, trust in algorithms is a self-fulfilling prophecy, working like a form of confirmation bias: for instance, online daters with high levels of trust in the algorithms of dating apps have a more positive experience at first dates, because they believe in the algorithm's ability to find their match (Sharabi, 2021).

This faith in algorithms might even lead to a sense of 'algorithmic providence' and serendipitous encounters, which have been called 'algorithmic conspirituality' (Shin et al., 2022), a belief that content is promoted to users in a knowing, almost cosmically ordained fashion by algorithmic intervention, rather than merely calculated inference. In other words, "people trust algorithms to tell them things about themselves that they cannot see" (3). Conspirituality substitutes divine intervention with an algorithmic recommendation. It is a form of alternative epistemology co-constituted with algorithmic actors, in which the hermeneutics of faith has as its locus the alleged revelatory powers of platforms themselves. On TikTok, for instance, users can be seen to attribute deep significance to content on their For You Page (FYP): "if the

FYP algorithm has displayed this video to you, it must be meant to be" (Cotter et al., 2022, 3). This line of thinking of course completely bypasses problematic aspects of algorithmic recommendation, the necessity and complexity of content moderation, and the regulatory and governance logics of platforms. When we are entering into debates and discussions on social media platforms, moreover, it is very easy to forget about their for-profit models, which naturalizes the private component of these spaces where supposedly public interactions are taking place.

In this section, we have established how trust in relation to people as well as texts and other cultural expressions is conditioned by online environments and how platforms enable and preclude trust relations and communities. We discussed a prevalent tension between private and public spheres and the need for interpretability to establish trust in platforms. We saw how, in spite of this need, there is a tendency to project agency and intentionality onto their algorithms. We now proceed to examine a case study from online culture from the perspective of the hermeneutics of faith and the contemporary phenomena of trust in algorithms and platforms, with an eye for the role of close reading and viewing practices.

He Said, She Said? Trusting Johnny Depp

Actors Johnny Depp and Amber Heard got married in 2015 and divorced a year later. Besides filing for divorce, Heard also got Depp a domestic restraining order. In 2018, she was interviewed for the *Washington Post* where she called herself "a public figure representing domestic abuse" (Heard, 2018). Although the article did not mention Depp's name explicitly, it was implied that he was the abuser, leading to the loss of his role as Jack Sparrow in the *Pirates of the Caribbean* franchise and his role in the Harry Potter prequel series *Fantastic Beasts*.[4] UK tabloid *The Sun* published an article calling Depp a 'wife beater,' which led him to sue the paper. Depp lost the case and filed a defamation suit against Heard in Virginia in 2022, claiming she was the abuser and suing her for 50 million in a civil case; Heard counter-sued for 100 million. In the end, the jury found both liable for defamation. Depp was awarded fifteen million dollars in damages and Heard two million. It has been suggested that the very different outcomes in the UK and US were at least partly due to the media event surrounding the US trial, which was live-streamed on multiple platforms. Over three million viewers watched the verdict on June 1, 2022.

On social media, fans closely watched and monitored the trial. They took pictures and edited their own short, decontextualized clips from these recordings which went viral on TikTok and Instagram. So-called 'fan-cams,' recordings taken and circulated by fans, were used to analyze every little detail of the polarizing trial, including both ex-partners' testimonies, behavior, and even what they were wearing. Interpretations based on these screenshots and clips were shared via Twitter/X, Reddit, and You-Tube. Fans thus engaged in hermeneutic activities, gathering and analyzing pieces of 'evidence,' including lots of misinformation and conspiracy theories around the trial: "Seeing themselves as citizen journalists or amateur detectives, social media users rework the truth according to their own belief systems, and present their interpretations as facts that are true, real and neutral" (Moro et al., 2023).

Remarkably, most of the audience that followed the trial through traditional and social media sided with Depp, to the bewilderment advocates of the #MeToo movement (with its call to 'Believe Women'), with respect to which the mediatized trial has even been said to constitute a "backlash" (Simic, 2022). On Twitter/X and TikTok, the hashtag #JusticeForJohnnyDepp got 15 billion views and #amberheardisaliar 1.2 billion, while #IStandWithAmberHeard only reached 44 million.[5] Depp's humorous replies to his interlocutors became taglines on t-shirts and shot glasses. Heard, on the contrary, did not receive much support. Social media portrayed her as manipulative, suggesting she used her acting talents to 'play' the victim. It has been noted that Heard's counter-violence makes her an 'imperfect victim' as opposed to 'the good victim,' which adds to the publics' readiness to take Depp's side (Harper et al., 2023).[6]

Both camps accuse the others of bias; both parties were accused of DARVO (deny, attack, and reverse victim and offender) tactics, when perpetrators of domestic violence "deny committing any wrongdoing, attack their victims' credibility, and cast their victims as the real aggressor and themselves as the real victims when held accountable or confronted with their abusive behavior" (Harsey & Freyd, 2020, 482). Whereas other studies have focused mostly on suspicion against Heard,[7] we chose to examine the role of trust, faith, and confirmation bias in the ways in which fans 'read' Johnny Depp's performance and public discourse. What is the foundation of fans' trust in Depp and how does it inform their strategies of close reading and viewing? In the scaled reading that follows, we turn to a dataset from the subreddit r/JusticeforJohnnyDepp, as well as images with the hashtag #JusticeforJohnnyDepp on Tumblr. How are hermeneutic strategies of close reading and viewing employed by fans to come to their own interpretation of the media event? We want to see how, a community of trust formed around Depp at this time, as well as if and how confirmation bias contributed to this.

Platform Hermeneutics

Here, we look at platform affordances in relation to specific modes of self-expression and word use, focusing on two platforms: Tumblr and Reddit. An overview of the platform affordances of Tumblr has already been given in Chapter 2. We assume that most readers will have heard of Reddit, a social news aggregation website that allows users to share and discuss web content about almost any topic. Reddit is divided into subreddits created by communities of users. Most subreddits are public; therefore, users are encouraged to use pseudonyms. Anonymity affords the freedom to share personal stories and express unpopular opinions, including politically incorrect remarks, a chance to say something but not be held accountable. It creates an environment where ideally, only the quality of arguments is used to persuade, rather than the user's credentials or authority in other spheres. But it also affords provocation and toxicity (e.g., swearing).

Posts and comments can be voted on by members of the community, determining their visibility, visible as a 'karma' score, which consists of the total of upvotes minus the downvotes. It is also important to note that on Reddit, users subscribe to content, rather than following members. Constraints to the discussion are posed by the platform architecture, particularly its code, which is non-transparent, yet determines the posts that are displayed in my feed and in what order, granting some posts more visibility than others according to an opaque logic. Still, Reddit's platform architecture lends itself more to democratic engagement than, for instance, Facebook's, because of its relatively open structure. In principle, all users can interact without necessarily having to follow each other or be on the other's friend list, as on Facebook. At least in theory, this improves the chance of a user being confronted with things that they do not already believe or agree with and thus it encourages debate and dialogue.

Reddit's two main personalization features, the ranking of content and its affordances for user interaction, are both strategies to counter information overload through filtering and distributed moderation (Pibernik, 2016). However, as an inadvertent side effect, they also potentially cause echo chamber effects, as has for instance been argued for r/The_Donald, a subreddit devoted to Trump support (Guest, 2018). Very broadly defined, an echo chamber "comes into being where a group of participants choose to preferentially connect with each other, to the exclusion of outsiders" (Bruns, 2017). Of course, we want to know whether that is also the case for the Subreddit r/JusticeforJD. The community has 51,000 members to date; it was created in February 2020, almost a full year after Depp began his lawsuit. The community's name and main description ("A community of people trying to provide facts as to why we support Johnny Depp")[8] make clear its intentions to foster participation among like-minded users and create an ingroup and outgroup mechanism.

When we look at its rules and regulations, we see that limits are being imposed as well, to warrant civil discussion and minimize toxicity, for instance prohibiting hate speech and misogyny and forbidding users to post things that are "vulgar or unnecessarily rude to others, whether it's another redditor, or AH herself"; "This isn't a battlefield for gender wars"; and "focus on the legal justice, not personal hate." Misinformation and conspiracy theories are also off limits, as is gaslighting. Finally, the subreddit's main purpose, as stated, is to "promote the truth, discuss evidence, and discuss the social impacts" of the trial. Joking and memeing should therefore be kept to a minimum.

Distant Reading

For our analysis on the scale of distant reading, we collaborated with Stefan Melis who created a script to crawl the subreddit r/justiceforJohnnyDepp. Unfortunately, we were not able to scrape all posts, comments, and replies through Reddit's Application Programming Interface (API), which only allowed us to extract posts going back to a certain point in time (December 20, 2022).[9] Each post was turned into one .json file and for each, we registered the same data regarding that post or comment: title, text, identifier, author, karma flair, collections of comments; we did the same for the comments (without 'title'). We then wrote a second script that takes those texts one by one and runs them through OpenAI's API, using the gpt-3.5-turbo model. The script runs through all the files and enriches them with so-called 'trust indicators,' signaling where topics related to trust are discussed. We designed a prompt for GPT, a natural language text with the following instructions:

> You are a skilled PhD student in social media studies and will be given tasks involving texts which have to be analyzed.
> You are a practical worker and you follow instructions to the letter.
> """"
> prompt_text = r""""
> **IMPORTANT: If the provided text is insufficient, unclear, or missing, simply return an empty array '[]'.**
> **IMPORTANT: Always return a complete array of JSON objects. Never end it with an ellipsis.**
> You're analyzing a series of texts related to the trial between Johnny Depp (often referred to as "JD") and Amber Heard (often referred to as "AH"). The texts are submissions and comments taken from the subreddit r/JusticeForJohnnyDepp on Reddit. The texts might contain profanities, memes, URLs, inside jokes, or other distractions. If the text contains only spam or an image, or if no text is provided, simply return an empty array.
> Your task is to identify indicators of trust or distrust towards Johnny Depp, Amber Heard, or entities related to them (e.g. family, lawyer, friend, colleague, etc.). Your response should be in the JSON format, and must be brief since it'll serve as input for a software application. Don't look for anything other than indications of trust or distrust.
> Your response should be one array containing individual dictionaries for each indicator of (dis)trust.
> For a single indicator:

```
```

[{"category": "trust", "towards": "Amber Heard", "why": "Expression of empathy", "relation": ""}]

For multiple indicators, all elements should still be in a single array:

```
```

[{ "category": "trust", "towards": "Johnny Depp", "why": "Positive endorsement", "relation": ""}, { "category": "distrust", "towards": "Amber Heard", "why": "Neglecting a perspective", "relation": "" }].[10]

Notably, the prompt needed repeated revisions: we needed to 'tell' ChatGPT very precisely what it needs to give us and how, and especially guide it in what *not* to do. The script developed and applied by ChatGPT then divided all the posts, comments, etc. in our dataset into two categories: *trust* and *distrust*. It also specified a 'towards' category, answering the question 'trust/distrust to whom?,' a 'why?' category with the reason for the (dis)trust, an optional category describing the relation of the person/entity named here if not Amber Heard or Johnny Depp. See Figure 3.1 for an example of what such an annotated post looks like. This way, it ran through the whole folder, file by file.[11] The program thus 'annotated' 637 posts and 17,694 comments. A look at the assigned trust indicators and relations will help us come to some preliminary answers to our question, what the public's overwhelming trust in Depp may be based on. Many of the posts categorized as trusting toward him mention the actor's public reputation and priors as the main reason. For instance, the fact that he has no known history of domestic violence, but also that he seems to be a civil person during the trial: "We see him in court, being a gentleman and talking to people." For posts in this category, parasocial relations are often of central importance, as fans attest to feeling like they know the actor intimately after having 'followed his career' throughout the years: "I've seen JD grow older in public for longer than she's been alive, and I read every tabloid headline about him and Kate Moss."

Besides reputation and priors and partially resulting from these parasocial relationships, some fans practice what we might call 'interpretive charity' toward their idol (Sperber, 2010, 585). This is a form of confirmation bias often

Figure 3.1 Example of annotated (and anonymized) post with trust indicators, object, and reason.

applied to the utterances of politicians, celebrities, and public intellectuals held in high regard by their audience, who are deemed authoritative on the issues they discuss. The more evidence is open to a variety of interpretations, the bigger the chance that obscure statements can inspire a response of interpretive charity, the tendency to explain an utterance in the most positive or meaningful way. This occurred when Johnny Depp attested to his drug abuse in the trial. Rather than making Heard's allegations of violent behavior more believable, for many fans on the subreddit, his confessions made him even more trustworthy, since "He doesn't pretend to be perfect." Moreover, it makes his story more coherent, hence convincing: "it makes sense that he breaks stuff, does stupid things and probably the fights aren't pretty and chivalrous."

Yet another way of 'knowing' that Depp speaks the truth is based on the actor's facial expressions, which are closely monitored and read throughout the trial, isolated through stills and clips and exposed to analysis: "I knew Johnny was telling the truth because any survivor of abuse could read the pain in his eyes." This could be seen as a form of 'conspirituality': one where it is not so much the algorithm, but the technologically mediated image that creates the effect of directly 'speaking to' and resonating with the viewer as a message addressed to her. A last finding we wish to include here is that the community displays a strong distrust of the mainstream media ("the media really is the opposition party"), as reflected in a number of posts. The 2023 Netflix documentary, which also considers Heard's side and especially goes into the abuse she suffered, is the latest target of this distrust.

We see that the method we used here for distant reading is a quick and easy way to visualize and categorize some of the main reasons for attitudes of trust and distrust toward several entities in a dataset. However, it also has some limitations. For one, the program as written now is still skewed toward trust: it will identify more relations as trusting than distrusting, sometimes wrongfully[12] and it tends to look for trust relations in a post or comment, even when there are none. An obvious solution to this problem would be to feed more content into the prompt for ChatGPT, in the form of exemplary cases, including more 'parent messages' (higher levels of embedding) as well as better samples.

Hyper-Reading with Imagesorter

In order to analyze images relevant to our case study, we extracted data from Tumblr. As explained in Chapter 2, Tumblr's platform culture is home to many fandoms and fan communities and its affordances enhance identification with content. Visual content is one of the platform's most compelling features, so we analyzed how images could be seen to boost trust or suspicion in the Depp vs. Heard case. We selected posts with the hashtag 'justiceforjohnnydepp,' which is the rallying cry of Depp defenders. To retrieve images from the platform, we used the Tumblr Tool developed by Bernard Rieder.[13] This Tumblr scraper retrieves co-hashtags and post data for a query of a hashtag.

The tool uses the 'Get Posts with Tag' script to retrieve metadata about posts with a certain hashtag. The search was fixed at 100 iterations, meaning that only up to 100 pages can be fetched; 20 posts are documented per page, giving up to 2,000 scrapeable results. Images from posts tagged with the hashtag were downloaded from the Tumblr tool's HTML output through the web extension 'DownloadThemAll.' Then, the 4,558 resulting photos were studied through Imagesorter which, as its name suggests, is an image sorting tool.[14] Imagesorter allows for the browsing of a high number of images and categorizes them by a chosen parameter. Sorting by color renders patterns visible, such as a high density of text images (like tweets), a particular trend, or a particular aesthetic. For this case study, we examine how Depp's image as a figure of trust was constructed aesthetically by his fans. In Figure 3.2, you see what the results from Imagesorter look like. The images are clustered together according to color and zooming in allows us to see what these clusters are composed of.

The biggest cluster in our results is the white one at the bottom right of the images. It is composed of court documents, social media communiques like the one Depp posted on his Instagram account following the verdict, screenshots of journalistic articles and thinkpieces, as well as social media sleuthing on Heard's profiles. The images in this cluster all favor one side of the story, with Depp's statement being the most present, meaning it was uniquely posted many times. However, we also see a deep engagement with facts and evidence presented in the trial itself, with many court documents posted and rigorously

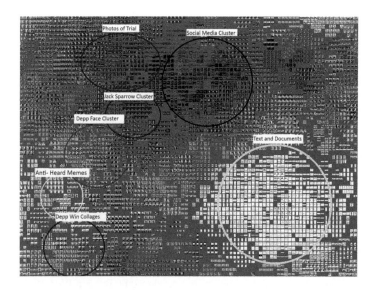

Figure 3.2 Imagesorter results clustered.

analyzed. A list titled "Remember what Amber Heard Did" numbers fourteen of Heard's abuses and is annotated with evidence naming the parties and witnesses involved. Users also track social media activity on both Depp's and Heard's accounts, screenshotting and annotating comment sections such as in Figure 3.3. Other images show a side-by-side comparison of which celebrities liked, respectively, Heard's and Depp's posts: an act interpreted as a measure of support.

In the black and white cluster (Figure 3.4), we find supportive collages of Depp with text such as "Congratulations Johnny Depp, justice has prevailed,"

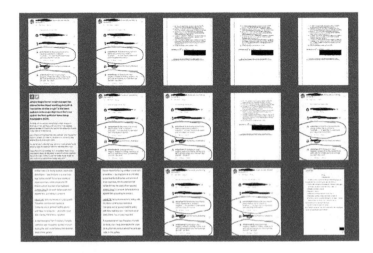

Figure 3.3 Social media sleuthing on Heard's accounts.

Figure 3.4 Supportive collages of Depp.

"he won," and "Tell the world Johnny." These are overlaid on serious, intense shots of Depp looking straight into the camera. The pictures chosen here imply trust between the viewer and Depp. Close-ups of a face can foster a sense of interconnectivity and reinforce parasocial relations. As Mary-Anne Doane (2003) writes, the close-up brings into play the oppositions between surface and depth, exteriority and interiority. It gestures to a beyond. The expressive face is a gateway to intersubjectivity: seeing it in close up, it is hard not to wonder what the person is thinking or feeling. Intimacy is thus built into these collages where Depp's face is the main feature.

The next cluster (see Figure 3.5) focuses on Depp and the roles Depp has played in order to establish him as a trustworthy party, such as Captain Jack Sparrow from the *Pirates of the Caribbean* franchise, Edward Scissorhands, or Cry-Baby. The photos are taken both from his public life and his film roles intermixed, showing us that his public persona heavily relies on his iconic roles, presenting him as a rebellious and misunderstood figure. The results from our dataset show us how fans forge a correlation between his personal attractiveness, the roles he played, and his estimated trustworthiness.[15] What

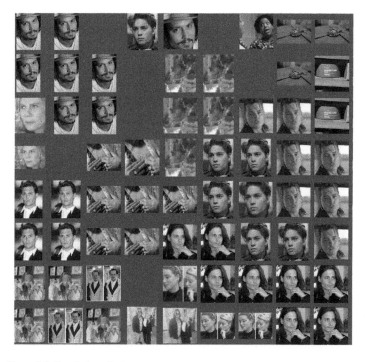

Figure 3.5 Depp's face cluster.

we see here is an instance of the 'halo effect,' where people come to an overall positive attitude toward a person based on one trait, which is automatically carried over to whole personality: "After the rater has cast a halo around his subject, he is dazzled by its radiance that he cannot differentiate the subject's separate qualities" (Johnson & Vidulich, 1956, 130). The halo effect is related to interpretive charity, it is a form of bias that makes fans trust or believe a celebrity due to their attractiveness and public image. In this case, fans see Depp as the admirable 'outlaw' characters he portrayed on films like Jack Sparrow, Edward Scissorhands, or Gilbert Grape and this somehow makes it impossible to conceive of him as someone capable of domestic violence.

Conclusion

As with the example of Trump's evangelical supporters, we see that the audience in this court case does not rely on intermediaries like traditional news outlets to interpret this event for them, but rather goes directly to "the source" to subject it to their own readings. We see that, instead of trusting mainstream media or going by the official interpretations of the legal professionals and journalists, fans often consumed the original source material. They parsed transcripts from testimonies in the trial, audio recordings of conversations that had been publicized, both ex-spouses' body language and clothing, stills from the broadcasting, etc. They close-read and view all this 'evidence' and come up with their own interpretations. To take part in such online communities takes up a lot of time and cognitive and hermeneutic effort. As Felix Brinker has written with respect to complex TV series, such fandoms demand a "meticulous, almost obsessive attention to detail and the readiness to engage in time-consuming and laborious close readings of scenes and even individual frames" (2013, 4). Advanced algorithms designed to feed them similar videos do the rest of the work by creating filter bubble effects. As a result, even though the court asked the jury not to read up about the case online, jurors were almost certainly exposed to the public opinion that was overwhelmingly in favor of Depp and shamed and discredited Heard.

Even though we analyzed this case study through the lens of trust, this 'he said, she said' shows that the hermeneutics of trust and distrust are really two sides of the same coin, they necessitate and perpetuate each other. In a polarized landscape, both sides suggest that *the other party* is either falling prey to being manipulated by the attention economy or strategically monetizing this situation, whereas they themselves can somehow rise above or stand outside it and know 'the truth' or 'what really happened.' They do 'the work' of hermeneutics for themselves: analyzing content like screenshots, stills, clips, and documents that seem to come directly from the source, but in reality are of course hypermediated. Fans experience this material as addressing them and revealing some direct truth about their idol, in a way that others—in this case, believers of Heard and the mainstream media—are somehow blind to. In these processes, platforms are still too often thought of as neutral facilitators of discussion and ways to access and share content, not as actively shaping these trust relations. Fans place a blind trust in Depp, but also in these online platforms. In the next chapter, we argue for the importance of situating the platform and its infrastructure within the process of dialogue.

Notes

1 They cite Paul de Man who argued that poetry is the "foreknowledge" of criticism and that the interpreter therefore "discloses poetry for what it is" and articulates "what was already there in full light" (Best & Marcus, 2009, 22; Paul de Man, *Blindness and Insight* (New York, 1971), 34; 31).

2 It needs to be said that the case studies that are often chosen to demonstrate these approaches are far from 'random' texts: we already know that a novel like *Beloved* does important critical work to offer an alternative take on ethics based on witnessing (and we would say we 'know' this precisely from earlier interpretations, which Love cites extensively).

3 It is, however, important to note that this trust varies according to levels of algorithmic literacy: people with lower algorithmic literacy are more suspicious toward search engines and more skeptical about the reliability of their results, while those with more online experience have more trust in their findings (Reisdorf & Blank, 2021).

4 UK fans denounced the involvement of actor Johnny Depp and campaigned for him to be removed from the franchise. After Rowling continued to support Depp, proceeded to hijack the franchise narrative by publicly shaming Rowling and the director for casting him (Driessen, 2020).

5 #amberturd had gathered 4.9 billion views on TikTok in February 2023; '#amberheard [??]' (195.5 million views), '#amberheard [??]' (30.2 million views); '#amberheardcrying' (1.3 million views) (Moro et al., 2023). Other popular hashtags include #AmberHeardIsALiar.

6 This, in turn, was criticized by feminists who supported Heard: in France, the new hashtag #MauvaiseVictime (bad victim) was introduced.

7 To name just a few: Valenti (2022) analyzes online memes and hashtags targeting Heard as an example of misogyny and shows how Heard's memeification was used to dehumanize her. Bot Sentinel Inc. (2022) conducted a quantitative analysis of tweets targeting Heard, which contain many ad hominem and antifeminist insults. Harper et al. (2023) have conducted a Critical Discourse Analysis of the case in news media, uncovering two main discursive strategies: (i) predication and argumentation and (ii) the construction of ingroups and outgroups. Strathern and Pfeffer (2023) use an automated toxicity identification tool to identify hate speech, toxicity, and impoliteness in the online discourse surrounding the trial.

8 Later it became "A community of people who support Johnny Depp's comeback after the Virgina trial" (r/justiceforJohhnyDepp).

9 Data were extracted using Reddit's API, dated from 20-12-2022 to 24-08-2023.

10 See complete prompt on https://www.ingevandeven.com/chatgpt-prompt-for-trust-analysis-r-justiceforjohnnydepp/.

11 The code is available in a github repository (https://github.com/smelis/trust), so you can use and adapt it for similar projects of your own. The development of trust and distrust toward entities over time would be an appropriate subject for further study; for instance, the effect of the trial's outcome or the 2022 Netflix documentary on public perception.

12 For instance, a comment marked as "'trust in AH" begins with "I believed Amber!", but then the poster states they were a victim of abuse themselves and therefore

inclined to trust Heard, only to later realize "she was lying" based on audio recordings and deposition videos. So in this instance, the program disregards the past tense of "I believed Amber" and then reads the whole comment as a statement of trust.

13 Rieder, Bernard, "TumblrTool" Github. Retrieved from: https://github.com/bernorieder/TumblrTool.

14 'Imagesorter' *Tucows Download*. Retrieved from: http://www.tucows.com/preview/510399/ImageSorter.

15 In addition to circulating flattering photos and fan montages of Depp, his fans also posted unflattering photos of Heard in what can be understood as an attempt to discredit her.

References

Best, S., & Marcus, S. (2009). Surface Reading: An Introduction. *Representations*, 108, 1–21.

Bot Sentinel, inc. (2002, July 18). Targeted Trolling and Trend Manipulation: How Organized Attacks on Amber Heard and Other Women Thrive on Twitter, *Bot Sentinel*. https:// botsentinel.com/reports/documents/amber-heard/report-07-18-2022.pdf

Brinker, F. (2013). Narratively Complex Television Series and the Logics of Conspiracy – On the Politics of Long-Form Serial Storytelling and the Interpretive Labors of Active Audiences. *"It's Not Television" Conference*, Goethe Universität Frankfurt/Main, Germany. Accessed through Academia.edu.

Brooks, C. (1947). *The Well Wrought Urn: Studies in the Structure of Poetry*. Eugene, OR: Harvest.

Bruns, A. (2017). Echo Chamber? What Echo Chamber? Reviewing the Evidence. In *6th Biennial Future of Journalism Conference* (FOJ17). Cardiff, UK.

Compagnon, A. (2014). The Resistance to Interpretation. *New Literary History*, 45(2), 271–280.

Cotter, K., et al. (2022). In FYP We Trust: The Divine Force of Algorithmic Conspirituality. *International Journal of Communication*, 16, 1–23.

Dahlberg, L. (2001). The Internet and Democratic Discourse: Exploring the Prospects of Online Deliberative Forums Extending the Public Sphere. *Information, Communication & Society*, 4(4), 615–633.

Dahlgren, P. (2005). The Internet, Public Spheres, and Political Communication: Dispersion and Deliberation. *Political Communication*, 22(2), 147–162.

De Man, P. (1971). *Blindness and Insight. Essays in the Rhetoric of Contemporary Criticism*. New York: Routledge.

Doane, M. A. (2003). The Close-Up: Scale and Detail in the Cinema. *Differences: A Journal of Feminist Cultural Studies*, 14(3), 89–111. DOI: 10.1215/10407391-14-3-89

Driessen, S. (2020). 'For the Greater Good?' Vigilantism in Online Pop Culture Fandoms. In Trottier, D., Gabdulhakov, R., & Huang, Q. (Eds.), *Introducing Vigilant Audiences* (pp. 25–48). Cambridge, UK: Open Book Publishers.

Empson, W. (1930). *Seven Types of Ambiguity*. London: Chatto & Windus.

Fawzy, N. (2018). Paul Ricoeur's Literary Hermeneutics and Biblical Exegesis. 7(3) هرمس 217–255.

Felski, R. (2015). *The Limits of Critique*. Chicago, IL: The University of Chicago Press.

Freelon, D. (2015). Discourse Architecture, Ideology, and democratic Norms in Online Political Discussion. *New Media & Society*, 17(5), 772–791.

Fuchs, C. (2014). Digital Prosumption Labour on Social Media in the Context of the Capitalist Regime of Time. *Time & Society*, 23(1), 97–123.

Grondin, J. (2015). Ricoeur: The Long Way of Hermeneutics. In Malpas, J., & Gander, H. H. (Eds.), *The Routledge Companion to Hermeneutics* (pp. 149–159). London and New York: Routledge.

Guest, E. (2018). (Anti-)Echo Chamber Participation Examining Contributor Activity Beyond the Chamber. *SMSociety*, 18, July 18–20, 2018, Copenhagen, Denmark.

Guest, E. (2020). Echoing Within and Between: Quantifying Echo Chamber Behaviours on Reddit. Doctoral thesis, University of Manchester. https://research.manchester.ac.uk/en/studentTheses/echoing-within-and-between-quantifying-echo-chamber-behaviours-on

Harding, S. (1996). Gendered Ways of Knowing and the "Epistemological Crisis" of the West. In Goldberger, N. R. (Ed.), *Knowledge, Difference, and Power: Essays Inspired by Women's Ways of Knowing* (1st ed., pp. 431–454). New York, NY: Basic Books.

Harper, E. I., Gibbons, D., & Bates, E. A. (2023). The Johnny Depp and Amber Heard Case in News Media: A Critical Discourse Analysis. *Partner Abuse*, 14(3), 291–316.

Harsey, S., & Freyd, J. J. (2020). Deny, Attack, and Reverse Victim and Offender (DARVO): What Is the Influence on Perceived Perpetrator and Victim Credibility? *Journal of Aggression, Maltreatment, & Trauma*, 29(8), 897–916. DOI: 10.1080/10926771.2020.1774695

Hayles, N. K. (2012). *How We Think: Digital Media and Contemporary Technogenesis*. Chicago, IL: University of Chicago Press.

Heard, A. (2018). I Spoke Up Against Sexual Violence — And Faced Our Culture's Wrath. That Has to Change. *The Washington Post*. Retrieved December 18, 2018. https://www.washingtonpost.com/opinions/ive-seen-how-institutions-protect-men-accused-of-abuse-heres-what-we-can-do/2018/12/18/71fd876a-02ed-11e9-b5df-5d3874f1ac36_story.html

Hill, K. A., & Hughes, J. E. (1998). *Cyberpolitics: Citizen Activism in the Age of the Internet*. Lanham, MD: Rowman & Littlefield.

Johnson, D. M., & Vidulich, R. N. (1956). Experimental Manipulation of the Halo Effect. *Journal of Applied Psychology*, 40(2), 130–134. DOI: 10.1037/h0042887

Karpf, D. (2012). *The MoveOn Effect: The Unexpected Transformation of American Political Advocacy*. Oxford: Oxford University Press.

Love, H. (2013). *Close Reading and Thin Description*. Durham, NC: Duke University Press.

Love, H. (2010). Close But Not Deep: Literary Ethics and the Descriptive Turn. *New Literary History*, 41, 371–391.

Manderino, M. (2015). Reading and Understanding in the Digital Age. A Look at the Critical Need for Close Reading of Digital and Multimodal texts. *Reading Today*, 22–23.

Marcus, S. (2007). *Between Women: Friendship, Desire, and Marriage in Victorian England*. Princeton, NJ: Princeton University Press.

Moro, S., Sapio G., Buisson, C., Trovato, N., & Duchamp Z. (2023). To be Heard through the #MeToo Backlash. *Soundings*, 2023(83), 90–101. DOI: 10.3898/SOUN.83.06.2023

OpenAI. (2023). OpenAI API with GPT-3.5-Turbo. [software/API]. http://openai.com/api

Pariser, E. (2011). *The Filter Bubble: How the New Personalized Web Is Changing What We Read and How We Think*. London: Penguin.

Reisdorf, B. C., & Blank G. (2021). Chapter 23: Algorithmic Literacy and Platform Trust. In Hargittai, E. (Ed.), *Handbook of Digital Inequality* (pp. 341–357). Cheltenham: Edward Elgar Publishing.

Ricoeur, P. (1970). *Freud and Philosophy: An Essay on Interpretation*. (D. Savage Trans). New Haven, CT: Yale University Press.

Ricoeur, P. (1976). *Interpretation Theory: Discourse and the Surplus of Meaning*. Fort Worth: Texas Christian University Press.

Ricoeur, P. (2007). *The Conflict of Interpretations. Essays in Hermeneutics*. Evanston, IL: Northwestern University Press.

Sedgwick, E. K. (2003). *Touching Feeling: Affect, Pedagogy, Performativity*. Durham, NC: Duke University Press.

Sharabi, L. L. (2021). Exploring How Beliefs about Algorithms Shape (Offline) Success in Online Dating: A Two-Wave Longitudinal Investigation. *Communication Research*, 48(7), 931–952. DOI: 10.1177/0093650219896936

Shin, D., et al. (2022). In Platforms We Trust? Unlocking the Black-Box of News Algorithms through Interpretable AI. *Journal of Broadcasting & Electronic Media*, 66(2), 235–256.

Simic, Z. (2022). Depp v. Heard: A Feminist Mea Culpa. *Lilith: A Feminist History Journal*, 28, 141–144.

Sontag, S. (2001 [1966]). *Against Interpretation and Other Essays*. New York: Farrar, Straus & Giroux. 3–14.

Sperber, D. (2010). The Guru Effect. *Review of Philosophical Psychology*, 1(4), 583–592. DOI: 10.1007/ s13164-010-0025-0

Strathern, W., & Pfeffer, J. (2023). Identifying Different Layers of Online Misogyny. Conference Paper. *arXiv preprint arXiv:2212.00480*. DOI: 10.36190/2023.54

Tripodi, F. (2022). *The Propagandist Playbook. How Conservative Elites Manipulate Search and Threaten Democracy*. New Haven, CT: Yale University Press.

Valenti, J., (2022, June 3). The Memeification of Amber Heard. *All in Her Head, Substack*. https://jessica.substack.com/p/the-memeification-of-amber-heard

Van de Ven, I. (2023). Attentional Modulation in Literary Reading: A Theoretical-Empirical Framework. *Orbis Litterarum*, 1–18. DOI: 10.1111/oli.12431

Van de Ven, I. (2018). Too Much to Read? Negotiating Legibility between Close and Distant Reading. In P. Hesselberth, J. Houwen. E. Peeren & R. de Vos (Eds.) *Legibility in the Age of Signs & Machines* (pp. 180–196). Leiden and Boston: Brill.

Wimsatt, W. K., & Beardsley, M. C. (1949). The Affective Fallacy. *The Sewanee Review*, 57(1), 31–55.

Wimsatt, W. K., & Beardsley, M. C. (1946). The Intentional Fallacy. *The Sewanee Review*, 54(3), 468–488.

4 Can We Talk? Dialogical Hermeneutics

Beyond Trust & Distrust

Steven Crowder's YouTube channel *Louder with Crowder* features a recurring item called 'Change my Mind,' in which the conservative political commentator and media host invites chance passers-by to debate hot topics with him. This often involves him sitting down at a college campus with his 'Change my mind' poster, depicting provocative claims like "Male Privilege is a Myth." Online, Crowder's sign was turned into a meme and quickly became a viral sensation (see Figure 4.1). As a meme, the Change my Mind format can be adapted to any outrageous proposition, with the aim to provoke the reader to debate and change the initial posters' mind.[1] What the memes really satirize here is a specific style of debate where one presents a solidly non-mainstream opinion in the form of a challenge and then triggers an interlocutor into doing the labor of countering this opinion. The style of communication that is mocked here is a confrontational and distinctly masculine one of being 'ready for debate,' competitive, opinionated, and devoid of emotion. The popularity of the meme shows how recognizable this style is in contemporary internet culture, which once again brings us back to the problems and challenges we started out with. This chapter entertains the possibility of other forms of communication in public online forums, conversations in which having one's mind changed is a real possibility and a two-way street.

Revisiting the state of trust in the information age that we outlined in the introduction to this book, we are again reminded of the importance of interpretation as a dialogical process. Are there ways to move beyond the stated dichotomy of (uncritical) trust and (unwarranted) distrust, which both often amount to having your mindset remain the same? Can we move toward new forms of intersubjective dialogue in online culture? In such a dialogical situation, ideally, the ideological distance between interpreter and text is not primarily an obstacle, but rather a source of productivity. But what could such a dialogue look like today? In online culture and as researchers in the Humanities, how do we see ourselves as interpreters co-produced alongside the materials we attempt to decode and make sense of? How do our prejudgments factor into our digital-hermeneutic readings? In this chapter, we look

DOI: 10.4324/9781003372790-5

Figure 4.1 Crowder's 'Change My Mind' sign memeified.

for answers by examining the subreddit r/changemyview. This is a discussion forum where users post their opinions while acknowledging that they might actually be wrong, with an openness to understanding alternative perspectives. How does dialogism come about on this public forum, and does it take us beyond the hermeneutics of suspicion and of faith? We assess the possibilities for epistemological border or horizon crossing in today's online public spheres in terms of a dialectical moment synthesizing trust and distrust.

Dialogue in Hermeneutic History

Although Gadamer is the most important proponent of dialogical hermeneutics, the concept of dialogue has a longer prehistory in the hermeneutic tradition. In the philosophy of Schleiermacher, the originator of modern hermeneutics, the notion of dialogue was already implicit in the mission of understanding the authorial intention, which urges the reader to go back to the original situation of discourse. And where Heidegger develops a hermeneutic phenomenology in *Being and Time*, he gestures toward the significance of dialogue in his section on discourse, which for him surpasses mere acts of stating: "it is the significant structuring of the intelligibility of our being-in-the-world" (Risser, 2015, 335). Our being with others also belongs to this phenomenon. Therefore, any form of discourse will always be an 'address' that is fundamentally aimed at communication. Discourse can make things manifest, thereby articulating a "being-with-one-another understandingly" (*Ibid.*). In this context, the act of listening becomes essential. When we aim at understanding through discourse, listening establishes the principal, authentic openness of Dasein to its own conditions of being. In listening to one another, 'being-with' unfolds. In Heidegger's later philosophy, listening to an address would take an even more prominent place.

Already in his early work, Gadamer was inspired by Heidegger's ontological hermeneutics to further develop his notion of a dialogue or conversation (*Gespräch*). For Heidegger, 'saying' always goes back to the 'speaking' of language itself and is thus impersonal. It answers to the event of Being in the call of language. In Gadamer's hermeneutics, by contrast, dialogue refers to an actual meeting or encounter. The meaning he assigns to this notion is, according to David Vessey, slightly different from our use of the word in everyday language, for it is more limiting. Going beyond a simple *exchange* (of viewpoints or pieces of information), a true dialogue is "the collaborative act of seeking to articulate understanding of a subject matter" (Vessey, 2012, 36). It belongs to the class of events that Gadamer calls 'play.' Playing together in a conversation is made into a central hermeneutic notion, which not only entails a submission of the individual to the rules of a communal undertaking but also harbors a realization of our freedom to be transformed and become more understanding. When performed correctly, such a dialogue or conversation allows the knower to come to an agreement with something other than the self, for instance a text or cultural object, and to achieve a view of the unity of its constituent parts. Dialogue establishes a particular conceivable manner of being with the other.

In *Truth and Method* (1960), Gadamer fully integrates the matter of dialogue and conversation into his hermeneutics. Here, he asserts that the (historical) object that we are trying to understand, which is always engrained in language and history, is only understood when confronted as 'thou':

> tradition is not simply a process that experience teaches us to know and govern; it is language— i.e., it expresses itself like a Thou. A Thou is not an object; it relates itself to us. ... For tradition is a genuine partner in a dialogue, and we belong to it, as does the I with the Thou. ... It is clear that the experience of the Thou must be special because the Thou is not an object but is in relationship to us.
>
> (1996, 358)

This way, he emphasizes that the text or object is never only theoretical, but relational—one part of an encounter with the interpreting 'I.' When the text is truly experienced as 'thou,' it makes a claim on the interpreter that is not to be ignored and cannot but be acknowledged. This is when listening occurs and a real dialogue ensues, enabled by openness to the other. This dialogue has the structure of questions and answers.

Questioning is not just an act undertaken by the interpreter but a two-way street; it is, in fact, the historical object that asks a question to the interpreter. In order to answer it, the interpreter, too, must pose questions. Questions are open ended, and thus one never knows beforehand where this conversation is going, but they are also restraining, because they are necessarily informed by certain presuppositions. Interpreters will thus be confronted with things that go against their own beliefs. Besides this structure of question and answer, a conversation requires that the interpreter is truly willing to understand. This means recognizing the value of the other, even where it opposes the self. More than an argument, a dialogue is of genuinely participatory nature and means a commitment to the event and the subject to that which emerges in-between interlocutors: "the more genuine a conversation is the less its conduct lies within the will of either partner" (Gadamer, 2004, 401). The aim is not mastery or control, but to take part in the other and share in its alterity: interpreter and text co-constitute each other, and reading is co-creation—an act that transforms both parties. This is a never-ending process, where the more a dialogue succeeds, the less it concludes, because ever new misunderstandings will come to light.

As pointed out in Chapter 1, Gadamer's hermeneutics has inspired later theories of race and gender in which dialogism also takes center stage. We see the notion of the horizon back in standpoint theory's insistence that the grounds for knowledge are intimately informed by history and society. Rather than pretending that knowledge originates under ostensibly universal conditions, feminist standpoint theorists refuse to perform the "God-trick" (Haraway, 1988, 581). They hold that it is inevitable that all knowledge-seeking and -producing projects are radically socially situated and then transform this situatedness into an accessible scientific resource. In *Visible Identities: Race, Gender, and the Self*, Alcoff draws on the insights of hermeneutic ontology to develop the idea of race and gender as social identities that function as interpretive horizons, embodied and situated systems of intelligibility within which understanding and meaning-making take place (Alcoff, 2006; Alcoff & Potter, 1993). Insisting that all knowing is situated, she sees the ontological prevalence that Gadamer gives to relationality as a feminist viewpoint (2003, 232). She values, amongst other features, the openness to alterity that is needed for Gadamer's hermeneutic dialogue and his move from knowledge to understanding (Alcoff, 2003, 256). However, she also critiques hermeneutics for its tendency to understate the importance of the *embodied* features of experience, especially vision and visibility. She therefore combines hermeneutics with phenomenology (simply put: the study of phenomena, or things that they appear). This way, she comes to an analysis of the ways in which racialized and gendered identities are materially manifested in the world. Alcoff takes the notion of the hermeneutic horizon to make explicit the epistemic effects of socially located differences. Identities function as horizons from which certain elements or layers of reality come to the fore. As a white woman, my knowing obviously comes from a different perspective than that of a black woman or a man. Differently identified individuals differ in their access to points of view that, in turn, may be relevant to the formulation of knowledge claims and theoretical analyses. What feminist standpoint epistemologies add to Gadamer's

hermeneutics is a sharper focus on the unequal power distributions in societies, as a result of which some groups and individuals are more inescapably
subjected to authority and tradition than others who come from positions of
privilege and domination. This does important work to nuance and diversify
the 'I-thou' relationship that Gadamer conceptualized, as well as the notion of
a dialogue. After all, it implies that we cannot take for granted that those who
enter into such a conversation are equal from the outset.

In addition to these standpoint theories, Fricker's theory of hermeneutical and testimonial justice also has important insights to add on the subject
of dialogue. We already briefly introduced her concept of hermeneutical in
Chapter 1, defined as the problem of significant parts of one's social experience being unavailable to collective understanding due to a bias in the collective hermeneutic resource of a given group (2007, 155). We mentioned the
#metoo movement as an example of bringing such formerly obscured experi-
ences to light. Groups that are excluded from understanding in this manner are
hermeneutically marginalized. Marginalized people suffer from a "situated
hermeneutical inequality" (162), which means that they are hampered from
making sense of experiences it is in their interest to make sense of. But besides hermeneutical injustice, Fricker distinguishes another form of epistemic
injustice that she calls testimonial injustice, which is just as relevant for our
reflections on the possibility of dialogue. Testimonial injustice describes a
situation where someone is being wrongly treated in their capacity as a *subject* of knowledge because of structural identity prejudices about the group
they belong to. Say, we lay out our line of argumentation in this book, but
as a reader you are reluctant to take at face value the idea that culture cannot
be studied with same objectivity as nature, and you explain the inclination
toward the 'soft' sciences and intersubjectivity as typical for female researchers. In such cases, a prejudice will stand in the way of the communicator being taken seriously as speakers and as communicators of knowledge, which
hinders their ability to contribute to the collective hermeneutic resource or
the pool of epistemic goods. Often, hermeneutic and testimonial injustice go
together, as when there is a lack of resources for a marginalized group to
share their experiences in an adequate manner and the resultant attempt at
expression reads as 'incoherent' and irrational, which is then chalked up to
the identity of that group.

In Gadamer's hermeneutics, prejudices are unavoidable; they can be obstacles but also productive to understanding. In epistemic injustice, prejudices
stand in the way, as our collective ways of understanding are structurally
prejudiced in terms of content, style, or both, as a result of which the experiences of the hermeneutically marginalized groups are left insufficiently conceptualized and understood, possibly even by their members themselves, or
their attempts at communication are heard or read as irrational because they
do not adhere to the dominant style. Fricker thus emphasizes the fact that the
traditions we inherited and that make up our fore-understandings are always

already (in)formed by power relations, misrepresentation, marginalization, stereotypes, and exclusions, and that this reinforces inequalities in society.

To address these wrongs, Fricker argues that a certain virtue is called for on the part of the addressee. In a sense, this addressee is also at a disadvantage in making sense of the other, as the hermeneutic resource lacks the tools to do so. However, Fricker argues for an intellectual virtue called hermeneutical justice as something that the hearer or reader can in such cases develop a sensibility toward. She defines this as a "reflexive critical sensitivity to any reduced intelligibility incurred by the speaker owing to a gap in collective hermeneutical resources" (7). The addressee is aware that the impediment to understanding the other's expressions might stem from a lack in the collective resources and consequently adapts their credibility judgment of the other's expressions in what we could call a more 'charitable' interpretation: "The guiding idea is to neutralize any negative impact of prejudice in one's credibility judgements by compensating upwards to reach the degree of credibility that would have been given were it not for the prejudice" (Fricker, 2007, 91–92). The listener recognizes that potential discursive incoherence, contradictions, and hesitancy stem from a lack in hermeneutic resources:

> an alertness or sensitivity to the possibility that the difficulty one's interlocutor is having as she tries to render something communicatively intelligible is due not to its being a nonsense or her being a fool, but rather to some sort of gap in collective hermeneutical resources. The point is to realize that the speaker is struggling with an objective difficulty and not a subjective failing.
>
> (Warnke, 2015)

If she has the time, the listener can then put more effort and attention into the dialogue by asking pro-active questions, also listening to what is not said; if she lacks the time, she is expected to reserve judgment regarding the speaker's credibility. Thus, Fricker recommends that we upwardly adjust the credibility of a speaker who suffers from identity prejudice in a move akin to Gadamer's fore-conception of completeness (formulating questions from the assumption that the expression is intended to be truthful and understandable). Even though Fricker lays more emphasis on power relations and identity prejudice, her account of hermeneutical justice aligns very well with Gadamer. Both think of listening and openness to the other as an ethical virtue and an epistemic demand (Warnke, 2015).

Deliberation

Before turning to an examination of the CMV subreddit, we here need to make a conceptual distinction between dialogue as outlined above and *deliberation*—a model for communication often used for the assessment of online debates. In political communication research, deliberation has a normative status. Although the two show considerable overlap, they diverge at important points. Deliberation is a form of debate that, amongst other qualities, "celebrates civility, reciprocity, openness, reason giving, and communication across lines of political difference" (Freelon, 2015, 773). A typical deliberative statement would be "I see your point, but nevertheless disagree completely" (civil disagreement) rather than "screw you" (a clear violation of the deliberative norm) (*Ibid.*). Like a dialogue, deliberation entails asking questions. It also includes giving reasons to support your views, a civil tone, and respect for those that think differently (Dryzek, 2001; Habermas, 1989; Mansbridge, 1983).[2] A difference is that deliberation aims more specifically at rationally motivated consensus, whereas a dialogue is more open ended. The reader should bear in mind that consensus is not the same as a true fusion of horizons.

Critics of Habermasian deliberative democracy have argued that its appeal to rational and reasonable argumentation reinscribes existing power relations: "reasonableness is itself a social construction that usually benefits those already in power" (Kohn, 2000, 409). Deliberation privileges the modes of communication of the elites and suppresses the reality of power relations. The 'rationalist bias' disregards a whole range of other modes that can be present in democratic discussions, such as affective, poetic, humorous/ironic modes (Dahlgren, 2005). We would argue that Gadamerian dialogue (complemented by feminist standpoint epistemology) does leave room for such modes of expression.

A last point to make before we go into our case study is that we should not envision the networked environment and platform infrastructure as neutral in facilitating dialogical interactions, as they actively shape (enable and constrain) certain modes of discourse. If we want to resist the naturalization of technology that we raised as a problem in Chapter 1, we need to be critically attentive to how the forms of deliberation available to us in our current platform ecosystem are essential to notions of trust and interpretation. In what follows, we therefore consider the difference between dialogue and deliberation in the context of (political) discussion on public platforms.

Changemyview: Dialogue or Deliberation?

> If you're here looking for capital-t Truth, you're already in trouble. The only thing this subreddit is good for is getting you to look at a question from an outside perspective. Persuasiveness is part of it, sure, but the ability to play devil's advocate is a feature, not a bug.
>
> Anonymous response on CMV, 2015[3]

Now let's see if we can update Gadamer's dialogical hermeneutics to the context of digital literary/media studies by looking at the subreddit r/changemyview.

As explained, Gadamer's main focus was on the historical gap between text and interpreter, but his dialogical approach has also been used for intercultural communication theories (e.g. De Mul, 2011). We believe his theory is just as vital for bridging epistemological differences in a contemporary context, especially in the face of polarization in online culture. The subreddit CMV was created in 2013 by a Scottish teenager called Karl Turnbull. As the story goes, he was searching for a place online where he and his friends could enter into meaningful discussions without being trapped in echo chambers and without rudeness, trolling, and people immediately closing off the conversation when a dispute arises (Chin, 2019). To Turnbull's surprise, such an environment was nowhere to be found; so he decided to create one himself, the subreddit CMV, where any topic is open for debate. The introductory description on the subreddit defines the forum as "[a] place to post an opinion you accept may be flawed, in an effort to understand other perspectives on the issue. Enter with a mindset for conversation, not debate" (website, "About Community"). CMV is "dedicated to civil discourse," with the underlying idea that "in order to resolve our differences, we must first understand them" ("What is r/changemyview?"). On the same page, it is noted that "productive conversation requires respect and openness" and that "certitude is the enemy of understanding" (*ibid.*). At the time of writing, the community has grown to 3.2 million members and has a strong community of moderators dedicated to enforcing the forum's rules and regulations. In 2019, Turnbull launched his own website based on CMV, www.changeaview.com, which takes the concept one step further, as it emancipates itself from reddit's infrastructure.

By now, CMV is well-known in academia as it has often been used as a case study for research on persuasion (Hidey et al., 2017), interaction dynamics (Jo et al., 2018), and attitude change, including argumentation techniques (Papakonstantinou & Horne, 2023; Priniski & Horne, 2018; Na & Dedeo, 2022), linguistic indicators of persuasiveness (Tan et al., 2016; Xiao & Khazaei, 2019), or the characteristics of posters who are susceptible to having their minds changed (Tan et al., 2016). The question we pose here is whether such a platform succeeds in facilitating real, mutual dialogue in the Gadamerian sense. In addition, we will see how we, as researchers, can enter into a dialogical relationship with the platform and its discourse.

Platform Hermeneutics

We have already discussed Reddit's platform architecture and specific technological and social affordances in the last chapter, so we can skip that level here and move directly to the subreddit CMV. The affordances of the platform are used by the subreddit's moderators to shape the interactions taking place in their highly controlled forum. These include pre-selecting desired content, the number of characters or words users are allowed or required to enter per post, the possibilities for commenting, and for reporting offensive behavior.

All these factors will shape the interactions taking place on the platform. As discussed, Reddit's most important personalization features, such as user interaction via distributed moderation and algorithmic content ranking, help users to not be bombarded with information by structuring and filtering it. However, as a side-effect, they also have the potential to generate powerful echo chamber effects. CMV has been described by researchers as a possible "way out of the echo chamber" (Guest, 2020; Pibernik, 2016).

As said, on CMV, users post their views on a range of issues and challenge others to change their minds in the comments. Users argue against the original poster's (OP's) view, posting persuasive messages. Responses usually share a line of reasoning, but they can also contain links to outside sources and statistics (Priniski & Horne, 2018). Commenter are asked to come up with arguments and be open to constructive discussions. Posts on CMV can be related to nearly any topic, but many of them relate to politics and an even larger number pertains to the parapolitical domain, meaning they may not deal directly with politics in a direct way but express societal topics that touch upon it (Dahlgren, 2005). At the time of writing, the all-time most popular topics include the following:

"Fat acceptance is the same as enabling an addict"; "If Trump gets re-elected, I have to accept that the people and the government have spoken and I am just incompatible with the US"; "Big Cruises do more harm than good, and the planet is better off if the industry dies or is overhauled"; "Arguments against universal healthcare are rubbish and without any logical sense"; "Tipping should not be expected for takeout orders" and "Statistics is much more valuable than Trigonometry and should be the focus in schools". (CMV; Top; All Time, 2023) There are certain rules in place that differentiate CMV from other subreddits and that are reinforced rather strictly. Original posters should be open to having their mind changed and they should make an effort to explain why they hold a certain view ("Rule A: Explain the reasoning behind your view, not just what that view is"). Importantly, they should *personally hold* the view and demonstrate an openness to having changed. However, what someone 'really' believes can of course not be checked. Because of the anonymous or pseudonymous nature of the platform, it is impossible to determine intent. This is where trust comes in. Original posts should be at least 500 characters long and topic openers agree to follow the conversation for at least three hours after opening the topic (Rule D); both of these rules make clear that the subreddit goes against the non-committal nature of many other online platforms and that is required of participants to make an effort in terms of time and attention. Likewise, a rule for commenters is not to post "low effort" responses. Importantly, users are not allowed to be "rude or hostile" to others, to accuse others of being unwilling to change their view, or of trolling (CMV, "Rules").

CMV's most important feature is that the community gamifies the process of view-changing by implementing an award mechanism called the delta system. Posters are asked to award a delta, which is a digital award, to commenters who succeeded in changing their view. For a delta, the comment must contain at least 50 characters; they must also add an explanation of why and how their view has been changed. The delta is then confirmed by the 'delta bot.' It is possible to award more than one delta within a single thread, and, besides OPs, commenters can also award them. The most persuasive users are ranked on the delta board on the subreddit's front page.

These rules are all designed to facilitate a productive debate, and they both constrain and afford an individual to develop a reasoning to support their view. We also see that CMV's specific rules foreground civil discussion and are in favor of a deliberation framework. The rules are enforced by volunteer moderators in accordance with the moderation standards as well as 'normal' users who tend to point out violations of the community guidelines. Human moderators make sure that original posters elaborate on their opinions, and that the discussion remains civil and articulate. Both official and unofficial moderators do this in their free time, with no financial reward. CMV's moderation is relatively strict, with prominent intervention being the norm, especially comment removal (after three subsequent comment removals, users are banned from CMV).

The Dataset

For the steps that follow, we scraped all comments and posts of a random month, February 2023, with the help of the open access tool Communalytics. The resulting dataset contains 1,742 posts and 28.258 comments—hardly big data, of course, but it would be too big of a volume to have to close read. First, we removed suspected bot accounts (382) by simply deleting all usernames ending in *bot. We also removed stop words. In total, 5,859 unique authors commented in the subreddit data. Approximately, 3.11% of all posts and comments (n = .934) had been deleted. Metadata include the name of the subreddit, author, text of each comment as well as the exact time and date it was posted. The dataset contains, among others, post titles and text as well as usernames.[4]

Distant Reading

For the scale of distant reading, we chose the Natural Language Processing (NLP) approach of topic modeling. This technique allows us to track down semantic patterns for our corpus. Topic modeling is a machine learning technique that automatically extracts topics from texts, searching for patterns of word use in a single text or corpus. Documents consist of multiple such topics, which we could see as 'hidden variables' reflecting their thematic structure (Van de Ven & Van Nuenen, 2022). A topic model is usually made bottom-up, not led by the semantic assumptions of the researcher, although it needs to be said that as soon as we start selecting and interpreting the model, these assumptions are brought back in, as we will see shortly. Moreover, the technique is 'unsupervised,' which means that it finds relationships between words without knowing what these words mean (Van Nuenen & Van de Ven, 2020). For our topic model, we used the tool Voyant, which is freely available and easy to use without necessitating programming skills. We prepared our corpus by removing all stop words and filtered for nouns. Next, we needed to determine the optimal number of topics. The number of topics that constitutes an accurate model can be tested by calculating coherence scores. The measure ('c_v') refers to the relative distance between words in a topic (meaning how often they appear together in documents). In our case, the optimal model we decided upon consisted of ten topics (see Figure 4.2).

As expected, we see the prominence of words associated with politics in several of the topics: words like 'candidate,' 'terms,' and 'vote.' However, our focus for this chapter is on the possibility of dialogue on a platform like reddit and in a community like CMV—a topic which certainly relates to but is not limited to politics. We therefore took an immediate interest in the topic that contained the word "wrong," hoping it might lead to examples in the corpus of people admitting to having their views changed or at least to instances of debate. We also suspected that the topic which included the word "believe" might be promising, even though it loads only 7.5%. We see that this is where the personal interests of the researcher come in, which, rather than a shortcoming of our method, is precisely the point: when we bring our expectations, biases, and prejudices into dialogue with the data, this will later bring our presuppositions into view and make our scaled reading intersubjective. All we know at this stage is that the term "believe" features prominently in a topic that somehow also relates to companies, deductions, and times, which is not

Topic	%
people lgbt community pay police tax becoming ranked could end	13.0%
anything candidates worse social money religion cant use practice matter	12.1%
corporations best employees representation something year automatically process new class	11.4%
feel really one completely candidate choice either problem terms showing	10.5%
us system tip work firefighters paying view culture officers similar	9.7%
would rcv media vote firefighter great society every pool fill	9.4%
wrong customers many college americans theyre used else often s	9.2%
support tipping problems voting done know gpt gets shit chill	9.0%
taxes officer ai argument others due countries returns ways yougov	8.3%
think companies using good company deducted depressed decided believe times	7.5%

Figure 4.2 Example of a topic model in Voyant.

very clarifying. For our next step, we retain the word to see if we can learn more about the ways in which these terms are used in particular instances in the corpus.

Hyper Reading

On the next scale, we are going to read (in a more traditional sense of the word) sentences surrounding terms that we have found ('local context,' in Gebaudo's [2016] terminology). Hyper reading is an umbrella term for non-linear, screen-based and computer-assisted modes of reading, including keyword searches, skimming, and scanning. It allows us to intuitively and associatively trace our own interests across the data set and thus helps us identify passages that contain significant features to then select for close reading. For this scale we use concordances, which trace keywords across the corpus back to their original lexical environments. This allows us to re-contextualize the potentially salient words identified on the previous scale (Van de Ven & Van Nuenen, 2022). We used Antconc—a freeware corpus analysis toolkit for concordancing and text analysis.[5]

First, we traced the word "wrong," selected at the distant reading level, back to its contexts of origin. As said, we expected it to signify instances where people admitted to having been wrong about something they previously believed in. Fittingly, this assumption itself turned out to be wrong, and we were confronted with our prejudgments. We see that more often than expressing faulty viewpoints, the word "wrong" was used to express moral judgments. Most often, it would be used in an expression of negation, prefaced by "nothing", for instance "There isn't anything inherently wrong with..."; "There is nothing wrong with... [a preference; having a one night stand; a racial identity, etc.]." This tells us that in addition to rationality and logic, morality plays a role in the discussions on CMV.

Our second term of interest was "believe"; in Figure 4.3, you see an example of a concordance view for the term in our CMV dataset. While we expected the word to lead us to examples where people express what they believe, with the possibility of having those beliefs transformed in conversation, what we find when tracing the word throughout the corpus is that it is also used in totally different contexts, which have to do with facts and proof. Such a foregrounding of factuality might be a direct result of the emphasis on rationality, civility, and deliberation that we also saw on the level of platform hermeneutics in the subreddit's rules, regulations, and moderation policy.

Close Reading

Our hyper reading then allows us to further zoom in toward 'telling' passages or samples with a high density of the words we deemed of interest, but this time traced back to their original context. For instance, when we traced the

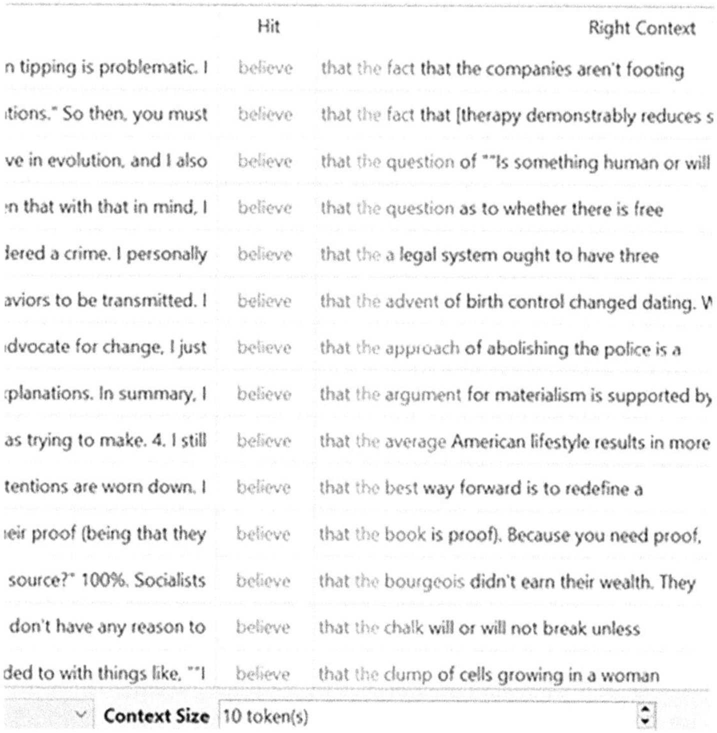

	Hit	Right Context
n tipping is problematic. I	believe	that the fact that the companies aren't footing
itions." So then, you must	believe	that the fact that [therapy demonstrably reduces s
ve in evolution, and I also	believe	that the question of ""Is something human or will
n that with that in mind, I	believe	that the question as to whether there is free
lered a crime. I personally	believe	that the a legal system ought to have three
aviors to be transmitted. I	believe	that the advent of birth control changed dating. V
dvocate for change, I just	believe	that the approach of abolishing the police is a
cplanations. In summary, I	believe	that the argument for materialism is supported by
as trying to make. 4. I still	believe	that the average American lifestyle results in more
tentions are worn down. I	believe	that the best way forward is to redefine a
ieir proof (being that they	believe	that the book is proof). Because you need proof,
source?" 100%. Socialists	believe	that the bourgeois didn't earn their wealth. They
don't have any reason to	believe	that the chalk will or will not break unless
ded to with things like, ""I	believe	that the clump of cells growing in a woman

⌄ **Context Size** 10 token(s)   ⬍

Figure 4.3 Concordance view of CMV corpus in Antconc.

words related to "believe" and "belief" in our corpus, this led us to a number of potentially salient posts, from which we selected one. This particular post was one in the "meta" category, meaning it is a post about the subreddit, titled "Using ChatGPT on CMV." At the scale of close reading, we examine the post more rigorously, with attention to the particularities of style as well as the role of emotion, ambiguity, irony, and other forms of tension. On the occasion of previous studies, this approach has proven fruitful for examining the linguistic characteristics of discourses on the Red Pill community on reddit and experiences of depression, respectively (Van Nuenen & Van de Ven, 2020; Van de Ven & Van Nuenen, 2022). In contrast to these discourses, the use of language on r/changemyview is remarkably (but unsurprisingly) unemotional, with a clear emphasis on deliberation, rational argumentation, and logical debate.

The OP asks whether a post generated by ChatGPT should be allowed on CMV. They themselves think the answer is 'no,' since the point of this subreddit is to post "what you believe in your own words." Therefore, they suggest a small amendment to the rules to be made to allow for the use of AI for part of a post, but only if it is openly disclosed and not counted toward the minimum character limit. The top response to this post considers both the pros and cons of including AI-generated text: "AI-generated text can provide a starting point for discussion on a topic that might not have been considered before," "suggest new perspectives or arguments that may challenge our existing beliefs and encourage us to think more deeply about a particular issue," and "help identify and address common fallacies or biases in arguments." In addition, it can "identify patterns of reasoning or language that may be misleading or illogical," leading to "more productive discussions where arguments are based on sound reasoning rather than flawed logic." At the end of this comment, it was revealed to be written with the help of ChatGPT. A respondent counters by saying that "When writing a reply, I have to consider whether you actually believe and can defend what you wrote," which would be incongruent in case of AI-generated text, which lacks intentionality. Another user points out they use the subreddit as a "mental gym" to "challenge [their] own beliefs as much as other peoples [sic]," to which someone responds that many users are part of the community to "win and farm karma." From this post and its thread of responses, it becomes clear that some users indeed foremost use CMV to hone their debating skills and improve their 'karma game,' their main goal being to persuade as many OPs as possible, almost regardless of the topic. Yet, there is also a group of users who do demonstrate the openness that is prerequisite for a dialogue. The community shows internal diversity in terms of uses and goals, even though we did not see much linguistic or stylistic variance. The latter can be explained by the relatively strict moderation policies and the aforementioned emphasis on civil, rational debate.

Conclusion

In the face of the increasing weight in Western culture of doubt, skepticism, and the overvaluing of independent truth finding, we follow Gadamer, Alcoff, and Fricker in underlining the importance of interpretation as a dialogical process. In our first chapter, we expressed a need for crossing epistemological borders. We can now see how spaces like CMV can be used to this end insofar as they pose a corrective to issues like polarization, biased content ranking algorithms, context collapse[6] and lack of privacy, abusive behavior, and a general lack of meaningful discussion in the online space.

However, we have also seen that because of the community's rules, strict moderation, and platform affordances, the emphasis is on deliberation, or civil, reasoned discussion, and that this mode is not always truly dialogical in the Gadamerian sense. The latter would imply listening to the other as an ethical imperative, even when this other is not able to adhere to the rules of civil discussion, for instance, because they are at an epistemic disadvantage as a result of unequal hermeneutic participation. In other words, the platform affordances preclude the necessity of hermeneutical justice, since signs of reduced intelligibility due to a gap in hermeneutic resources may be preemptively weeded out. It is one thing to assume the fore-conception of completeness or genuine intent in the case of a speaker who adheres to these rules, but quite another thing to extend the same courtesy to someone who appears incoherent or irrational. Arguably, understanding is even more urgent in the latter case.

Furthermore, a true dialogue succeeds all the more the less it comes to a close. The delta stamp could be seen as a way to close the hermeneutic circle. Granted, it is possible to award several deltas in one discussion thread and, by extension, to keep changing one's mind. But as we have seen, on CMV, it is not always clear whether commenters are also participating with an openness to change their views, or whether this fore-conception of completeness is rather a one-way street. Interestingly, it was precisely the thread on bringing AI into the mix that sheds some light on these questions. It seems that some users indeed foremost use CMV to hone their debating skills and up their 'karma game' by persuading as many OPs as possible, while others demonstrate the open attitude that is prerequisite for a dialogue. In this respect, the subreddit is not a unified, homogeneous community.

Another possible downside of the platform's infrastructure when it comes to dialogue is the fact that the delta award is in effect rather binary: you either have your own view changed or not. The same goes for Reddit's system of upvotes (for a comment you agree with) and downvotes (when you disagree). This does not allow for a lot of nuance, for instance, the nuance of taking the other seriously as if their argument was in itself complete and understandable, without necessarily subscribing to it completely or even agreeing. On the website changeaview.com, the up- or downvote is replaced with the option to award a shine, to flag an 'illuminating' comment that 'shines a new light' on the topic. This way, it is possible to indicate that your view might not be changed so much as modified.

Perhaps the most important insight to be derived from our case study is that we see how this online community is actively shaped by the rules of the platform. This case drives home that to believe in online dialogue, we should be able to trust in the wider systems in place that allow for a democratic discussion. To take at face value the exchanges generated on platforms is to ignore the more subcultural and subversive approaches toward creating content online. In understanding intersubjective dialogue as something that just 'happens' on online platforms, we place too much trust in the forms of platforms to stabilize discussions between equals. In reality, they are far from mere backdrops or neutral facilitators. We underline the importance of situating the platform and its infrastructure *within* the process of dialogue. Platform algorithms rank, distribute, and organize conversations. Their moderators censor, control, and regulate the topics. This techno-hermeneutic assemblage of human actors and technical affordances privileges certain tones and rhetorical styles over others. As we have seen, a digital-hermeneutic reading can situate our analyses of these discourses firmly in a critical examination of the platform architecture that affords them.

Notes

1 https://imgflip.com/memegenerator/Change-My-Mind.
2 By comparison, a communitarian norm for discourse adheres to the same rules, but only for those in the 'in-group'; according to the libertarian-individualist norm, insults are permissible, as is self-expression without listening to the other (Freelon, 2015).
3 Response to a post titled "CMV: The people with the most deltas are the worst people to listen to" (2015).
4 The metadata available through reddit's API include subreddit, author, and text body of each comment as well as the time and date it was posted. Many other variables are available in the dataset as provided by Communalytics, such as the score of a comment or the unique identifier of the original post on which it was made. Since these additional variables were not required for our inquiry here, they were not used in data collection.
5 https://www.laurenceanthony.net/software/antconc/.
6 Social media pulls different audiences from various networks and situates them in one place (boyd, 2008; Marwick & boyd, 2011), leading to ambiguous audiences (Davis & Jurgenson, 2014; Litt, 2012). Moreover, online communication can be asynchronous as internet users are not obligated to provide immediate responses, eliminating the temporal restraints of communication and allowing users to conflate different interactional contexts.

References

Alcoff, L. (2003). Gadamer's Feminist Epistemology. In Code, L. (Ed.), *Feminist Interpretations of Hans-Georg Gadamer* (pp. 231–258). Philadelphia: Pennsylvania State University Press.

Alcoff, L. (Ed.). (2006). *Identity Politics Reconsidered*. Berlin: Springer.

Alcoff, L., & Potter, E. (Eds). (1993). *Feminist Epistemologies*. London and New York, NY: Routledge.

boyd, d. (2008). *Taken Out of Context: American Teen Sociality in Networked Publics*. Dissertation. University of California, Berkeley. DOI:10.2139/ssrn.1344756

Chin, C. (2019, April 6). Change My View' Reddit Community Launches Its Own Website. *Wired*. https://www.wired.com/story/change-my-view-gets-its-own-website/

Dahlgren, P. (2005). The Internet, Public Spheres, and Political Communication: Dispersion and Deliberation. *Political Communication*, 22(2), 147–162.

Davis, J. L., & Jurgenson, N. (2014). Context Collapse: Theorizing Context Collusions and Collisions. *Information, Communication & Society*, 17(4), 476–485.

De Mul, J. (2011). Horizons of Hermeneutics: Intercultural Hermeneutics in a Globalizing World. *Frontiers of Philosophy in China*, 6(4), 628–655.

Dilthey, W. (1966). *Gesammelte Schriften (1914–2005)*. Göttingen: Vandenhoeck & Ruprecht.

Dryzek, J. S. (2001). Legitimacy and Economy in Deliberative Democracy. *Political Theory*, 29(5), 651–669.

Freelon, D. (2015). Discourse Architecture, Ideology, and Democratic Norms in Online Political Discussion. *New Media & Society*, 17(5), 772–791.

Fricker, M. (2007). *Epistemic Injustice: Power and the Ethics of Knowing.* Oxford: Oxford University Press.

Gadamer, H. G. (2004). *Truth and Method* (2nd ed., D. G. Marshall, Trans). London and New York: Continuum.

Guest, E. (2018). (Anti-)Echo Chamber Participation Examining Contributor Activity Beyond the Chamber. *SMSociety*, 18, July 18–20, 2018, Copenhagen, Denmark.

Habermas, J. (1989). *The Structural Transformation of the Public Sphere.* Cambridge, UK: Polity Press.

Haraway, D. (1988). Situated Knowledges: The Science Question in Feminism and the Privilege of Partial Perspective. *Feminist Studies*, 14(3), 575–599.

Heidegger, M. (2010). *Being and Time* (Macquarrie, J. Trans). New York: State University of New York Press.

Hidey, C., Musi, E., Hwang, A., Muresan, S., & McKeown, K. (2017, September). Analyzing the Semantic Types of Claims and Premises in an Online Persuasive Forum. *Proceedings of the 4th Workshop on Argument Mining* Copenhagen: Association for Computational Linguistics (pp. 11–21).

Jo, Y., Poddar, S., Jeon, B., Shen, Q., Rosé, C. P., & Neubig, G. (2018). Attentive Interaction Model: Modeling Changes in View in Argumentation. *arXiv preprint:1804.00065.*

Kohn, M. (2000). Language, Power, and Persuasion: Towards a Critique of Deliberative Democracy. *Constellations*, 7, 408–429.

Litt, E. (2012). Knock, Knock, Who's There? The Imagined Audience. *Journal of Broadcasting and Electronic Media*, 56(3), 330–345. DOI: 10.1080/08838151.2012.705195

Mansbridge, J. J. (1983). *Beyond Adversary Democracy.* Chicago, IL: University of Chicago Press.

Marwick, A. E., & boyd, d. (2011). I Tweet Honestly, I Tweet Passionately: Twitter Users, Context Collapse, and the Imagined Audience. *New Media and Society*, 13(1), 114–133.

Na, R. W., & DeDeo, S. (2022). The Diversity of Argument-Making in the Wild: from Assumptions and Definitions to Causation and Anecdote in Reddit's 'Change My View'. *Proceedings of the Annual Meeting of the Cognitive Science Society*, 44(44), 969–976.

Van Nuenen, T., & Van de Ven, I. (2020). Digital Hermeneutics and Media Literacy: Teaching the Red Pill across Horizons. *Tilburg Papers in Culture Studies*, paper 241.

Papakonstantinou, T., & Horne, Z. (2023). Characteristics of Persuasive Deltaboard Members on Reddit'sr/ChangeMyView. *Proceedings of the 45th Annual Meeting of the Cognitive Science Society*, 45, 3710–3717. https://escholarship.org/uc/item/6h12t1vd

Pibernik, M. (2016). Participatory Culture and Deliberation: Case Study of ChangeMyView. Universidad Carlos III de Madrid. https://www.researchgate.net/publication/313243019_Participatory_Culture_and_Deliberation_Case_Study_of_ChangeMyView

Priniski, J. H., & Horne, Z. (2018, July). Attitude Change on Reddit's Change My View. In *40th Annual Meeting of the Cognitive Science Society* (pp. 2279–2284). Cognitive Science Society.

Risser, J. (2015). Dialogue and Conversation. In Malpas, J., & Gander, H. H. (Eds.), *The Routledge Companion to Hermeneutics* (pp. 335–344). New York and London: Routledge.

Schleiermacher, F. (1988). *Schleiermacher: Hermeneutics and Criticism and Other Writings* (Ed. Bowie, A., & Clarke, D. M.). Cambridge, UK: Cambridge University Press.

Tan, C., et al. (2016, April). Winning Arguments: Interaction Dynamics and Persuasion Strategies in Good-Faith Online Discussions. *Proceedings of the 25th international Conference on World Wide Web*, 25, 613–624.

Van de Ven, I., & Van Nuenen, T. (2022). Digital Hermeneutics: Scaled Readings of Online Depression Discourses. *Medical Humanities*, 48(3), 335–346. DOI: 10.1136/medhum-2020-012104

Vessey, D. (2012). Gadamer and Davidson on Language and Thought. *Philosophy Compass*, 7(1), 33–42.

Warnke, G. (2015). Hermeneutics and Feminism. In Malpas, J., & Gander, H. H. (Eds.), *The Routledge Companion to Hermeneutics* (pp. 644–659). New York and London: Routledge.

'What is r/changemyview?' (2017). r/changemyview Wiki. *Reddit*. https://www.reddit.com/r/changemyview/wiki/index/#wiki_what_is_.2Fr.2Fchangemyview.3F

Xiao, L. & Khazaei, T. (2019, July). Changing Others' Beliefs Online: Online Comments' Persuasiveness. *Proceedings of the 10th International Conference on social media and Society*, 92–101.

5 Conclusions

We started out this book by outlining a number of issues related to trust in our information age with its many competing narratives and misleading information. At this time, deciding what sources and voices to trust becomes a particularly vexing matter, given limited resources of time and attention. Do our built-in cognitive mechanisms for 'epistemic vigilance' (Sperber et al., 2010) suffice to help us calibrate trust and distrust in content, authors, and platforms? In the digital humanities as well as digital culture at large, we signaled a prevalent tension between the subjective and the objective. This tension plays out as an ongoing preoccupation with the lure of 'dataism' or the Big Data Myth, while methods of filtering all this information may lead to selective exposure to content, making us astutely aware of the limited, situated, specific horizon of the individual. Throughout this book, we argued that this tension between seemingly objective and subjective content manifests as a problem of excessive trust in media platforms and likeminded others and excessive distrust of people who think differently.

To counter both these excesses, we stressed a need for epistemological border or horizon crossing previously pointed out by danah boyd (2018). Confronted with increasing polarization, ideological segregation, and a suspension between objectivity and subjectivity with little middle ground, our book argued for a renewed emphasis on interpretation, understanding, and intersubjectivity. Both in digital culture and in academia, as researchers but especially as teachers, what we need is the ability to understand views that differ from our own. The crisis we face today, boyd believes, takes place not at the level of facts, of what is true, but of epistemology: how we know whether something is true. This requires a cultural transformation of "how we make sense of information, whom we trust, and how we understand our own role in grappling with information" (boyd, 2017). Why do people with different worldviews interpret the same data differently or have altogether different views on what constitutes a fact in the first place? As Haraway writes, "Facts are theory-laden; theories are value-laden; values are story-laden. Therefore, facts are meaningful within stories" (1989, 79). Our challenge is therefore to lay bare these stories and help students understand epistemological differences, instead of transmitting received ideas on what is right or wrong. As

DOI: 10.4324/9781003372790-6

educators, we need to be able to teach across epistemologies and viewpoints. To this end, we proposed to update the hermeneutic tradition, with its emphasis on mediation, for the context of digital culture.

Chapter 1 therefore brought the long history of European hermeneutic thought—from Schleiermacher to feminist standpoint epistemology—into dialogue with present-day issues related to trust and distrust in media and its users. We tried to reposition hermeneutic thought for the digital and (according to some) post-critical or post-hermeneutic age, and made a claim for its relevance for problems of digital trust, fake news, and bias today. Hermeneutic theory and praxis, we argued, can help us mediate between concepts of objective reality and the subjective and limited nature of human experience by proposing a mode of intersubjectivity. They amount to a mediation between familiar and strange—not just historically or geographically, but also culturally and ideologically. Our approach to 'scaled reading' practices of digital culture consists of a reconfiguration of the hermeneutic circle. The movement from part to whole and back is here understood as a reading on different scales, from platform hermeneutics to distant reading, via hyper reading to close reading. The approach describes a circular structure or feedback loop that vacillates between the 'N = all' perspective of the whole (although for the sake of repeatability, we never actually used 'big data' in our case studies) and a close reading of the part or sample. Such an approach allows us to discern patterns in large-scale textual corpora, while also zooming in on the linguistic nuances of individual discourses. It emphasizes the importance of interpretation as a dialogical process.

Chapter 2 examined practices of suspicious hermeneutics in times of fake news and omnipresent deception in and through media. We have seen that uncovering hidden power structures and ideologies entails a substantial investment in terms of time, attention, mental energy, and hermeneutic activity. In this context, close reading and close viewing are an indispensable and invaluable part of citizen's media literacy, but they are often used for 'paranoid' ends when truth-seeking becomes a personal responsibility embedded in a culture of doubt and critique. Proposed solutions to fake news as a crisis in knowledge often revolve around introducing fact-checking and other verification tools like content moderation, but alternative knowledge infrastructures can also supply their own fact-checking, because they construct their own ecosystem. Most problematically, fact-checking could imply that there is an objective truth that should be established, and that deviations from this account can be understood as "fakeness," reinforcing a binary conception of truth. Most often, debunking fake news only serves to reinforce user's prior held beliefs. Indeed, the true/false dichotomy fails to render the way in which enunciations are solidified by the work of all sorts of actors (Latour, 2004) and 'facts' are built by a complex work of 'truth-grounding' (Lynch, 2005). Instead, we argued, we should understand that truths are environmentally constituted and culturally situated.

We demonstrated this by honing in on memes. Meant to travel and to be recontextualized, memes exemplify Ricoer's notion of meaning as multiple and the need for interpretation in online culture. Memes, irony, and trolling all transform notions of legibility and necessitate new forms of literacy. Whether an image is read as ironic is dependent upon context and audience. This also makes memes weaponizable: ironic jokes can become convictions, and memes start to have offline consequences. Right-wing discussion platforms use weaponization to strategically deny any real involvement with far-right ideas. The situation can become dangerous when "interpretation and judgement are evaded through tricks and layers of metatextual self-awareness and irony" (Nagle, 2017, 31). This way, extremist political positions have been able to infiltrate and thrive in the mainstream of online discourse through the trojan horse of memetic imagery. We argued that interpretation should not stop at the level of the text or image but should take platform culture into account, which we demonstrated through our exemplary reading of a toxic depression meme.

As this example showed, interpretation can mean unmasking or unveiling in a movement of demystification and the destruction of illusions. Yet, it can also entail the restoration of meaning, a revelation. In the case of a hermeneutics of faith, we saw in Chapter 3, the reader feels herself addressed by the text as if it was a message sent specifically to her. For Ricoeur, Heidegger, and Gadamer, interpretation was not just an epistemological exercise or a mode of knowing but also, or primarily, an ontological one, a mode of being. Rather than a reconstruction of the text's original meaning or the author's intention, this mode of interpretation revolves around self-understanding—understanding the self *through* the text. Even Bible exegesis was already a reflexive exercise in which the reader learned something about herself; each reader derived a different meaning from the text which could be related to her own situation in the here and now. This approach seems to bypass intermediaries to let the source speak in a direct manner and therefore often goes together with strategies like close reading and viewing. Close reading centralizes attention, patience, and the assumption of meaning as multiple. We argued that, used in the context of faith hermeneutics, it facilitates the 'revelatory' nature of the encounter between reader and text or image. In this way, trust and attention go hand in hand, just like distrust and close scrutiny.

But it is not just reading and viewing strategies that form communities of faith or trust. Today, platform infrastructure feeds into this. The notion that the text or cultural object is a message intended specifically 'for you,' we could say, has now become infrastructurally supported! We trust in the structures of platforms, often even blindly. Online echo chambers and algorithmic biases lead to a pervasive influence of confirmation bias and filter bubbles, amounting to the reinforcement of subjective worldviews. Through increasing integration of digital platforms into our personal lives and society (direct democracy, working from home, etc.), the aspect of mediation escapes our notice. In its stead, we get the appearance of directness and lived reality. To counter this, we have argued, the design of digital technologies should be emphasized as a field of mediation that shapes sociotechnical structures of interpretation. Rather than accepting this naturalization of the role of technologies in interpretation processes, we examined what forms of deliberation and dialogue our current platform ecosystem affords, and how these in turn inform our notions of trust and interpretation. How does the naturalization of the role of technology in communication influence hermeneutic practices?

Chapter 4 therefore positioned the difference between dialogue and deliberation within a consideration of platforms and publicity. The internet is disseminated into different spaces where rules for interpretation vary according to infrastructural and cultural grammars. Platforms construct new ways to read and interpret, each with their own set of deliberative parameters. This chapter first endeavored to update the notion of interpretation as a dialogical process of epistemological border-crossing. After examining the subreddit r/ changemyview as a case study, we reflected that such spaces can to some extent be seen to facilitate this dialogical process by countering (or minimizing) polarization, algorithmic bias, context collapse, toxicity, and abusive behaviour. However, we also stressed the importance of noticing the difference between dialogue and deliberation, where the latter emphasizes civil, reasoned discussion, rather than truly listening to the other *as other*. To be able to trust in the possibility of a genuine online dialogue, we concluded, we first should be able to trust in the wider ecosystems for a democratic discussion. After all, platforms are far from neutral facilitators of intersubjective encounters; a digital hermeneutic approach should therefore situate platform infrastructure within the process of dialogue.

Closing the Circle (For Now)

We hope to have convincingly argued throughout this book that hermeneutics can and should play a crucial role in digital humanities and literary and media studies today, that the hermeneutics of suspicion and the hermeneutics of trust can be used as lenses to examine online dynamics, especially on social media, and that dialogical hermeneutics can be seen as a productive response to excessive suspicion and excessive faith online. Our scaled reading approach integrates method and data on the one hand and interpretation on the other, making explicit how the personal interests of the researcher inform every step or scale of reading: our expectations, biases, and prejudices are brought into dialogue with the data, which brings them into view and allows for a mode of intersubjectivity. Thus, we can trace our own interests as researchers, be confronted with them, and have the data speak back.

Understood this way, science communication could also benefit from the insights of hermeneutic research, especially regarding the value of dialogue for forging trusting relationships with society. When it comes to scientific research, the Covid pandemic has shown there is a lack of trust from society amongst certain communities, which of course closely relates to the overwhelming volumes of misinformation and conspiracy discourse often referred to as the 'infodemic.' A survey among the Dutch public by the Rathenau Institute showed that transparency is a reason to trust science, but distrust emerges when transparency reveals disagreements between scientists. This stems from, but also feeds into, a tendency of scientists to "cultivate certainty and downplay disagreement" (KNAW, 22). The report advises academics to be open and transparent about what they do not know, which would not be harmful to public trust, and to stick to their own expertise, refraining from "epistemic trespassing" (Ballantyne, 2019). Faced with skepticism, scholars often respond by doubling down on a dichotomy between facts and values and a general belief that if only the public had a better understanding of facts, apart from worldviews, they would be trusting. Yet, the way in which people think and act in relation to their trust in research findings is not purely based on facts but closely interrelated with their norms and values, ideologies, worldviews, relationships, networks by meanings which are thoroughly social:

> building trustworthiness in modern society requires a fundamental shift from a 'let-me-explain-it-once-more' repertoire or a debate mode to a sustained dialogue in which the interplay between morality and science can be openly examined, questioned and discussed.
>
> (KNAW, 2022, 24)

All of this should drive us to rethink science communication as more than just explaining and presenting research findings to a larger audience. We must enter into dialogue with a sensitivity to underlying values and assumptions—in short, to different horizons.

The same goes for the field of education from primary to academic levels. boyd (2018) makes a case for helping people understand their own psychology. Students can learn to interpret media from multiple perspectives, when we help them see how they fill in gaps when presented with sparse information, and how they are influenced by prior beliefs and biases. We could for instance show how in case of a 'data void,' we start filling in the gaps through speculation, gathering crumbs of information and piecing them together (Golebiewski & boyd, 2018). This can "help students recognize their own fault lines, not the fault lines of the media landscape around them," make them aware of how interpretation is socially constructed and of how these constructions can be manipulated (2018). We believe that these are essentially hermeneutic goals, and that our approach to scaled reading can aid in achieving them.

As a last point to emphasize, more than we see happening at present, we can use a wealth of hermeneutic strategies and approaches from the tradition of literary studies to make sense of digital culture, coming to creative readings that combine close, distant, platform-oriented, hyper, paranoid, surface, and restorative modes of reading. Our scaled readings of visual-textual cases studies from contemporary online culture can be seen as a modest attempt to inspire students to try out such readings. They drew out the complexities inherent in adapting hermeneutics to the digital and are repeatable for a variety of online contexts. We therefore end by offering three suggestions of case studies for further application, which can be used in academic educational contexts like undergraduate courses. Adapted this way, hermeneutics could play a crucial role in digital humanities and media studies today.

Case Studies

Jordan Peterson and Interpretative Charity[1]

As you have read in Chapters 2 and 3, in some cases, 'old' practices of close reading and technological affordances that lead to echo chamber effects come together. One of these cases is the following of the Canadian public intellectual and psychology professor Jordan Peterson, whose popularity is partly due to his clever use of media. Peterson uploads his YouTube videos to his account with over 7.5 million subscribers and knows how to optimize and spread content, using, for instance, Instagram stories to alert his fans to new videos of him uploaded by other accounts. Content-wise, he taps into popular items in the media system like political incorrectness or anti-SJW and knows how to work YouTube's algorithms, which are known to prioritize niche, anti-mainstream, extreme, polarizing, and conspiratorial content. Once these are normalized, the user is nudged toward more edgy and radical content, creating social, political, and epistemological filter bubbles (Covington et al., 2016). Peterson's fans increase his visibility by uploading videos with hyperbolic and aggressive titles like 'Angry Jordan Peterson TRIGGERS French Journalist'; 'Jordan Peterson Destroys Islam in 15 Seconds'; 'JP Calmly dismantles feminism infront [sic] of two feminists.'[2] Such a framing of his media moments makes his fandom into a counterpublic to 'mainstream SJW discourse,' united in a reactionary position: opposition to feminism, social justice, globalism, 'cultural Marxism,' and left-wing politics in general (Van de Ven & Van Gemert, 2022).

However, if we want to fully understand Peterson's status as intellectual guru, we also need to take into account his writings and how his admirers interpret these. The notorious ambiguity and obscurity of these writings, often far from easily comprehensible, is repeatedly judged as 'profound' by his fans who are already in awe of him—a case of what cognitive scientist Dan Sperber (2010) has called the 'Guru Effect.' We could see this as an extreme version of the hermeneutics of faith. Uttered by already trusted speakers, obscure statements can inspire a response of interpretive charity (Sperber, 2010, 585). This principle is also notable in Peterson's reception, where critiques of his ideas only solidify his followers' beliefs. Devoted listeners and readers often end up paying more attention to confirming than disconfirming evidence, and strengthening their initial beliefs becomes a self-fulfilling prophecy. The effect of this confirmation bias is a powerful echo chamber. Taking together the writings and public appearances of Peterson (or another intellectual guru) with fans' interpretive activities on a public platform and applying the scaled reading approach presented in this book could offer valuable insights in the workings of confirmation bias.

Taylor Swift's Fandom

This case study is a bit similar to Britney Spears' vigilant fandom that we briefly described in the introduction to Chapter 3, with the difference that here fan activity is not carried out from a place of suspicion. Swift's eager and tight-knit fanbase, also known as 'Swifties,' are known to perform investigative work as part of their relationship to their idol, unpacking and decoding the many "Easter eggs" she leaves in her work. Indeed, speculation is key to building fan relationships, and Swift encourages it by incorporating hints and clues in her work that only a deeply invested Swiftie will have the know-how to unpack. Easter eggs originally described secret features in video games but have now become widespread in many forms of contemporary media. Hidden messages as ways to communicate with fans encourage close readings and viewings; interpreting them has become a staple in fan communities. Nowadays, YouTube videos unpacking "every easter egg you missed" in the latest blockbuster franchise film pop up on the platform shortly upon release, and avid fans walk you through all the references a casual viewer would not have the background to pick up on as something relevant to the story.

In Swift's case, these Easter eggs come in the form of symbols in her music videos, public appearances and interviews, lyric booklets, and other allusions in her songwriting that create a deeply intertextual body of work. Swift even stated in an interview that fans can either have a "normal" relationship to music, or: "If you want to go down a rabbit hole with us, come along, the water's great" (Grady, 2022). On Reddit, fans write that "Easter eggs are one of the most fun parts of being a Swiftie" and that they "never get old," because there is always a new way to interpret them. It seems that it does not matter if Swift stops incorporating Easter eggs in her work—fans are not going to stop speculating. However, for some Swifties, this has gone too far. Now, any of Taylor's public appearances are heavily scrutinized, from her outfit choices down to her nail polish color, everything is interpreted as a hint for what is coming next in her discography. In these interactions, the body of the celebrity is read as a public text begging to be deciphered. Possibly taking Spears' fandom as a counterpoint, our scaled reading approach can be applied to a dataset of choice on a platform and community devoted to Swift, asking at what point a playful hermeneutics tipples over into suspicion and conspiratorial thinking.

AI Images

The rise of artificial intelligence (AI) has led to all kinds of new challenges related to interpretation. AI has been embraced and lauded as a technology with the potential to change the world, but there are very significant consequences for our interpretive horizons if we continue to let AI-produced texts and images drip into our reality. AI images specifically are made to blend seamlessly into our world and are eagerly taken up by social media users and passed around, often without awareness they have been produced by generative AI. To understand how we should treat AI-generated images, we need to understand how they are produced. AI-generated images are made by machine learning algorithms using either a diffusion generative model or a generative adversarial network (GAN). A diffusion model elaborates parameters it has been given (a prompt) and a GAN pits two neural networks against each other to generate and evaluate images until it arrives at the desired result. In either case, AI is given an instruction or equation to solve, and uses the data it has been trained on to find the answer to the question. AI, in other words, calculates statistical probability. Art theorist and film scholar Hito Steyerl has called this mass-producing the "mean" image out of a dataset (2023). How can we interpret such images and to what extent does our existing hermeneutic toolkit fall short?

AI design researcher and media artist Eryk Salvaggio (2022) argues we should look at AI images as giving us information about the dataset such models have been trained on. In this way, they should be understood not so much as images but as infographics. This helps us identify the underlying biases of generative models. Studying images as the results of datasets thus helps to find what is in the dataset and what is not. For example, certain models produce inaccuracies or unrealistic depictions, meaning that the basis for the depiction was not included enough in the dataset for the model to be able to produce it accurately. Salvaggio found that to be the case for the faces of black women and for lesbian couples kissing. Whilst studying the output of a model called StyleGan, he found that the faces of black women were produced much less often than other genders and races, and that when they were, they were distorted or not convincingly human (2019). This led him to investigate the dataset the model had been trained on, where he found that black women only represented 2.55% of the data and, "by comparison, there were 1,152 white women, or 28.8%." It is vital to keep asking these questions when we study and interpret AI images online, because it enhances our literacy. We have to understand that these generative models do not create anything new out of a set of existing data, but only produce an average of what has been given to them, which implicates human creators as well. In this context, we can wonder if (or to which extent) it is legitimate to attribute to digital technologies or at least to an emerging part of them—an autonomous interpretational agency. Machine learning algorithms have already been considered as (a responsible) moral agents. Is there any room here for what might be called a nonanthropocentric or posthuman hermeneutics? For further study, you can look for an existing collection of AI images or curate one yourself.[3] You can then apply our scaled reading approach to try and see if you can get any information about what kind of dataset these images have been trained on to map out the prejudices of the generative model. Applying a symptomatic reading, keep an eye out to what is excluded from the images, in addition to what is included.

Notes

1 This case study has been previously published in Van de Ven & Van Gemert (2022) which you can consult for more details.
2 All uploaded to YouTube: DannyDoherty (2018); @acts17apologeticsdavidwood77 (2018); RobinHoodUK (2018).
3 You can find existing collections at a repository like Impossible Images: https://impossibleimages.ai/. Alternatively, you can use a text-to-image model like Dall-E 2 or Midjourney to render your own images: see https://openai.com/dall-e-2; https://www.midjourney.com/home?callbackUrl=%2Fexplore.

References

Ballantyne, N. (2019). Epistemic Trespassing. *Mind*, 128(510), 367–395. DOI: 10.1093/mind/fzx042

boyd, d. (2017). Did Media Literacy Backfire? *Journal of Applied Youth Studies*, 1(4), 83–89.

boyd, d. (2018, March 9). You Think You Want Media Literacy… Do You? *Zephoria*. https://www.zephoria.org/thoughts/archives/2018/03/09/you-think-you-want-media-literacy-do-you.html

Covington, P., Adams, J., & Sargin, E. (2016). Deep Neural Networks for YouTube Recommendations. *RecSys*.

Golebiewski, M., & boyd, d. (2018). Data Voids: Where Missing Data Can Easily Be Exploited. *Data & Society*. http://cognitionandculture.net/wp-content/uploads/Data-Voids.pdf

Grady, C. (2022, October 19). Let's Go Down the Rabbit Hole of Taylor Swift Conspiracy Theories. *Vox*. https://www.vox.com/culture/23411001/taylor-swift-conspiracy-theories-midnights-karma-is-real-gaylor

Haraway, D. (1989). *Primate Visions: Gender, Race and Nature in the World of Modern Science*. New York and London: Routledge.

KNAW. (2022). *The Pandemic Academic. How COVID-19 Has Impacted the Research Community*. Amsterdam.

Latour, B. (2004). Why Has Critique Run Out of Steam? From Matters of Fact to Matters of Concern. *Critical Inquiry*, 30(2), 225–248.

Lynch, M. P. (2005). *True to Life: Why Truth Matters*. Cambridge: MIT Press.

Manderino, M. (2015). Reading and Understanding in the Digital Age. A Look at the Critical Need for Close Reading of Digital and Multimodal Texts. *Reading Today*, 22–23.

Nagle, A. (2017). *Kill All Normies*. Online Culture Wars from 4chan and Tumblr to Trump and the Alt-Right. Winchester: Zero Books.

Noble, S. U. (2018). *Algorithms of Oppression. How Search Engines Reinforce Racism.* New York: New York University Press.

Salvaggio, E. (2022, October 2). How to Read an AI Image. *Cybernetic Forests, Substack.* https://cyberneticforests.substack.com/p/how-to-read-an-ai-image

Salvaggio, E. (2019, October 4). This Black Woman Does Not Exist. *Cybernetic Forests, Substack.* https://www.cyberneticforests.com/news/this-black-woman-does-not-exist

Sperber, D. (2010). The Guru Effect. *Review of Philosophical Psychology*, 1(4), 583–592. DOI: 10.1007/ s13164-010-0025-0

Sperber, D., Clément, F., Heintz, C., Mascaro, O., Mercier, H., Origgi, G., & Wilson, D. (2010). Epistemic Vigilance. *Mind & Language*, 25(4), 359–393.

Steyerl, H. (2023, March–June). Mean Images. *New Left Review*, 140–141, 82–97.

Tenen, D. (2017). *Plain Text: The Poetics of Computation.* Stanford, CA: Stanford University Press.

Van de Ven, I., & Van Gemert, T. (2022). Filter Bubbles and Guru Effects: Jordan B. Peterson as a Public Intellectual in the Attention Economy. *Celebrity Studies*, 13(3), 289–307. DOI: 10.1080/19392397.2020.1845966

Index

Note: *Italic* page numbers refer to figures and page numbers followed by "n" denote endnotes.

For Product Safety Concerns and Information please contact our EU
representative GPSR@taylorandfrancis.com
Taylor & Francis Verlag GmbH, Kaufingerstraße 24, 80331 München, Germany

www.ingramcontent.com/pod-product-compliance
Ingram Content Group UK Ltd.
Pitfield, Milton Keynes, MK11 3LW, UK
UKHW021112180425
457613UK00005B/54